FROM BOY TO MAN

FREDERICK ROGERS

Published in Australia by Sid Harta Books & Print Pty Ltd,
ABN: 34632585293
23 Stirling Crescent, Glen Waverley, Victoria 3150 Australia
Telephone: +61 3 9560 9920
E-mail: author@sidharta.com.au

First published in Australia 2021
This edition published 2021
Copyright © Frederick Rogers 2021
Cover design, typesetting: WorkingType (www.workingtype.com.au)

The right of Frederick Rogers to be identified as the
Author of the Work has been asserted in accordance with the
Copyright, Designs and Patents Act 1988.

All rights reserved. No part of this publication may be reproduced, stored in a retrieval system, or transmitted, in any form or by any means without the prior written permission of the publisher, nor be otherwise circulated in any form of binding or cover other than that in which it is published and without a similar condition being imposed on the subsequent purchaser.

Rogers, Frederick
From Boy to Man
ISBN: 978-1-925707-63-2
pp212

As you pass through these silent pages
Of hardships, joy and pleasure
Your heart will surely yearn for
The boys who won back your leisure

ABOUT THE AUTHOR

Frederick Rogers grew up in Wales U.K. and migrated to Australia after WWII where he married and had three daughters, one granddaughter, and two great granddaughters. He settled in Sydney N.S.W. where he has worked and lived for the majority of his 95 years.

CONTENTS

MY WAR FROM WARWICK FARM	1
A TRAINEE AT HMS *RALEIGH*	5
NORTH SEA COMMAND	15
TO THE FIORDS OF NORWAY	25
THE *ADMIRAL VON TIRPITZ*	33
I LEAVE THE *FURIOUS*	49
EMBARKATION LEAVE	65
I SAIL WITH THE *DOMINION MONARCH*	75
FIRST VOYAGE TO AUSTRALIA	83
GOLDEN HIND	91
HMS *ILLUSTRIOUS*	97
PACIFIC WARFARE	103
FONAP	117
HMS *COMET* AND HONG KONG	123
REMINISCING ABOUT AN EVENT ON THE *FURIOUS*	131
COMET CROSSES 'THE LINE'	133
TO WESTERN AUSTRALIA	139
MY FREE PASSAGE TO AUSTRALIA	149
FOLLY LOST	189
IN AUSTRALIA	193

MY WAR FROM WARWICK FARM

There I was, standing close to the replica of Sydney Harbour Bridge. I gazed at the huge expanse of Warwick Farm Racetrack as my mind floated back to 1945. I had been shipped out of the devastated world of war in the United Kingdom on a ship that was to be known as HMS *Golden Hind*. The establishment known to Sydney as Warwick Farm had been allotted to the British Navy as a dropping-off place for members of the British Navy awaiting orders to join the ships' crews.

How those years flooded back to me now as I looked around. For one thing, there was no Peter Warren car sales yard. In those days, there was no Masterton display village, and not even an eat-out place. No motel either. But there was a railway track running into the racetrack grounds. In 1945, Warwick Farm was simply Warwick Farm.

I watched the stream of traffic on the highway. How the flow of traffic had increased to this day in modern Sydney. The only thing that had not really changed was the railway establishment beside the rail track running into the racecourse. I stood there dreaming, and withdrew into a faraway shell. I remembered being at the crossroads of my young life in the midst of a terrible world war, and indeed racing out of control.

A small hand suddenly squeezed mine and I looked down at my granddaughter who was just six years old.

Her name is Casey and she's the daughter of my own daughter, Janet. In those days, it seemed a practice for grandparents to help out by minding the offspring's children while they needed to work. The squeeze of her hand brought me back to why we were at Warwick Farm in the first place. Casey had been waiting too long standing there when she could have been inside the display village looking at the nice houses. We had journeyed from Chester Hill on the short trip by electric train and the outing was a kind of break from playing schools together in my garden in Chester Hill. And by the way, when we played, I was always allotted the role of teacher's helper. Who do you think was the teacher? Casey brought me back to reality by looking up and asking me why I looked so sad.

My eyes glanced over towards the racecourse again and I tried to explain why this place, where we were standing, brought back so many good and bad memories. But just like a child, all Casey wanted to do was get on our way, so on our way we went. For that brief moment, the hint of war lifted my mind and I suddenly picked Casey up and hugged her so very tightly.

At the entrance to the display centre, I put Casey down and we moved into the building. There was a transparent floor where we could look down at the fish that were swimming in a pond beneath us. Casey was delighted. I was amazed at the string of words she came out with — she was determined to ask Daddy to come and bring his fishing rod with him. What would I say about that?

With the inspection completed, we got back to the train where my mind returned to the crossroads again. There I was, about to leave school whilst men and boys were marching off to war. This lay heavily on my mind. I was too young to volunteer and the war was at its deadliest. Should I take a job for the time being, or stick my head in the sand and pretend I would actually be allowed to join the forces? Reluctantly, I took a job at the local railway station where I became a telephonist and number-taker. Part of my job was to check up on wagons that were on loan to the coal mines and record the numbers of the wagons. But at the back of my mind was the day I would be allowed to join the Navy. I made up my mind to join the Navy as soon as I turned eighteen.

Tales of death and destruction filled me with guilt and despair. I sought the wisdom of my father and hinted to him how much I yearned to join the fight. I mentioned how people, innocent people, were being killed, homes and towns wiped off the face of the map. Men and women, not much older than I was had gotten into the battle to free the world from that tyrant, Hitler. Mates were out there battling for their country, and all I was doing was roaming the hills and dales collecting stupid numbers from wagons. My father listened and studied my determined expression. I knew I had to say much more, so I reminded him of my brothers doing their bit for King and country, and the fact that the war had already killed one of my brothers in that blasted air raid. I didn't intend to let that spark of determination die out in my soul. My dad kissed me on the forehead and gave his blessing if that was what I wanted.

Straight after my birthday, I was sent away to Newport where the big bosses ruled the roost. I put my story of need to them, and, fearful of the outcome of their wrong answer to my plea, I claimed I could not do my proper job in the company if my mind was on the war. I even told them I was determined to avenge the death of my brother in the Coventry air raids. That was a case of being in the wrong place at the wrong time. My brother's wife was in hospital and the hospital had suffered a direct hit. My brother was helping to evacuate patients from the building. His wife was saved, but he was killed by another direct hit. With this personal tragedy boiling in my blood, this trip had to be made. But looking at the row of glum faces before me, I wondered if I had bitten off more than I could chew, so to speak. I was asked to wait outside the boardroom, which I did until one of the group came out and told me to return to work while the decision was pending. It took a full week before the decision was reached, and when it was reached, I was released for call up into the Navy.

The time between my leave from my job and the actual day of my departure into the Navy seemed like a lifetime. Work seemed a drudge; answering phones and whiling away hours checking on railway wagons became a nightmare. When the nightmare ended, I was ready to leave for my new life.

A TRAINEE AT HMS RALEIGH

The morning of my departure for the training base was, for me, a continuous wave of excitement. My heart told me I was about to shake off my youth. I felt my old life slipping away. The sense of duty was stirring my blood to boiling point, but at the back of my mind was the feeling of sadness.

Leaving the family behind was something I had never done before. I could see how they tried to hide their own sadness at my trotting off into the wide, wide world. I was secretly glad when the time actually came for moving off. The family took their leave but remained in the kitchen as I made my way to the front door. It was my sister who came to the front door to see me off. I shall never forget the sad expression on her face as we parted. I made my way to the corner of the street a short distance away and turned to wave goodbye. We each threw a kiss and I left her standing there in the doorway of the house. Three weeks as a trainee, I thought to myself as I made my way to the station. Three weeks and maybe I could have a little leave, or should I call that shore leave? I should be home again before I was given a ship, but all this time meant I wasn't exactly part of the war. But the saying goes, 'Rome was not built in a day' so I must be as patient as God will allow me. I had another thought as I went on my way: maybe I could be home for Christmas as a very ordinary seaman.

I was at last on my wartime adventure. I was hoping my small part in the dreadful war would be of help in some way. My destination at this point was Plymouth, and the train journey was uneventful. The thought of setting foot in this famous town gave me the greatest feeling. Navy personnel were there to check out the other lads who were on the same train as I was. Protocol was the order of the day. I was glad to see so many other lads on their way to becoming sailors. A number of trucks and buses were on hand at the station to convey the lot of us to the Royal Navy training barracks — HMS *Raleigh*. I'm glad to say a fine meal awaited us on arrival, then we were off to the living quarters.

The living quarters turned out to be long wooden huts. I scored hut number fifteen with a few of the other lads, and as life would have it, we all got down to asking each other's names, what town we had come from and if there were any girls left home on hold. What an expression! Reminiscing was the main topic of conversation until into the hut entered the Petty Officer. He was the first officer with whom we had direct contact. He gave us a stern warning that 'lights out' would be at twenty-two hundred hours. I did a very quick calculation of civvy time and made it ten o'clock. He added that we should 'Hurry it up, my hearties' before leaving us to individual conversations. Sure enough, lights went out at the given hour.

The first night away from home felt just a little strange. My mind turned back to the family home, and thoughts of our parting eventually floated into waves of tiredness.

The morning heralded a brand new life, and the very early

morning found us being taken around the camp and lining up for medical examinations. Then, the event of extreme importance: the fitting of uniforms and kit issue, including a very funny item called the 'housewife', which turned out to be our salvation in the form of repair work on clothing and whatnot. A factor that needed to be carried out on uniforms above and beneath.

There was also another factor which we had to learn at times as it was the motto of all sailors — take orders and keep your mouth shut. Some of the lads thought this saying was a bit below the belt, but they were to soon learn it was best to obey orders and get on with the war. Civvy life was going to be a thing of the past.

Routine for the first of us trainees came to an end without too much harsh harassment. Bells at sixteen hundred hours — life in the Navy and loving it. Teatime came and went. Duty watches came and went, but reminiscing about home life continued long after close of day.

The lads who were posted on the same watch as me got together and we took to sharing our shore leave together — sometimes it was sightseeing, movies, or dances. It all came under our days off. But we could not escape the sadness on the faces of people around the streets. Plymouth had been another city badly hit by air raids.

The war was never far away, but we did manage the first traineeship with most of us filling our heads with thoughts of things to come on our horizons. But the following Monday morning we really got down to serious training. Book manuals to try to tackle with vigour. Reaction to navigation rules. The names of the parts of a ship. Green for starboard, red for port. The world of ammunition was overawing — huge guns, rifles, everything tuned in strictly for war. Days and weeks seemed to come and go at will. Fire watching became part of life. Air raid drill became second nature. We became quite prepared for any emergency, night or day. Frosty nights seemed to be kinfolk to enemy bombers. Death and destruction were part of life. Lighthearted moments came only when new recruits arrived. We oldies were cheeky enough to call them rookies — after all, we were sailors of three weeks standing. Most of us thought we deserved the right to call all newcomers rookies! Could anyone imagine us lot, with only a few weeks behind us as being sailors, calling the newcomers rookies? Our cruel onslaught didn't stop there, we pulled no punches as we continued our evil ways. We repeatedly told them that after they had been in camp a few days, the petty officers and officers alike would be on the lookout for guys who played games close to the wind. Guys who thought it was one big joke. This kind of mug intended to have a good time whilst hiding under the cloak of a uniform. These ratings were soon singled out and dealt with, but there were some lads I just had to be sorry for.

One day, this lad collared me on the parade ground. He asked me if it would be alright if he didn't have to march about the parade so much. He said he would be very pleased if I could give him advice — I really never got much chance to speak with him about it because he was suddenly called over by the duty officer to explain why he was wearing a pair of civvy shoes — that was something I hadn't noticed. I did hear the officer shout loud enough though. But I did have to smile at the boy's answer: apparently the poor lad had an ingrown toenail. It wasn't doing him any good with footwear the Navy dished out. I held my breath waiting for the outcome. The poor lad stood stiffly to attention as he was ordered to get himself to the sick day at the double. With his sore foot, he was going at a snail's pace. But that wasn't the end of it. As the lad made his way across the parade ground, the petty officer bellowed not to let the doctor cut the foot off. It must have sounded like doomsday to the lad because he fell into a faint right there on the parade ground. Me, being close at hand, had the job of bringing the poor kid back to life and carting him off to sick bay.

Such is life in the Navy. I cannot really remember if I ever saw the lad again. Life seemed to fly away so fast, and there were my orders to keep concerning becoming a true-blue sailor. That diversion seemed to be a bit of a break for me, which was good because for a short while I could put the raging war in the world on hold. That did sound strange, but if it was not for the air raids, the war could have been thousands of miles away. But the dark early nights were slowly creeping up on us. It was October and we had been at the barracks a whole three weeks. Needless to say, we were all doing our turns at fire watching and air raid drills. We were quite prepared for any emergency. The thought of shore leave at times lightened the load a little.

The cold and frosty nights approached with the chance of snow, which in turn, made me begin to think of Christmas. Would there be Christmas leave? This was on everyone's mind. We were not told about leave for the holidays. News began to buzz about, that maybe some of us would be drafted to ships before Christmas. Gunnery practice soon put our minds on other matters. Racing around from one end of the guns to the other, one minute I was ammunition number, then range finder — each guy taking turns — everyone becoming an expert at each point in case of accidents to any member of the crew. We thought it a bit funny at first, dashing around from pillar to post, but practice makes perfect and we all got on well together. We were all growing very fast and the thought some of us were about to lead a very dangerous life made me think of how many of we lads were not here today. Suddenly, halfway through a practice shoot, the gunnery officer told us he had something to tell us about leave. I almost dropped a shell, but we managed to complete our round and then waited for the gunnery officer to continue his great news.

The excitement that followed was great beyond words. We stood there smiling until we began to worry him to death to get on with his news. And it was great news. I thought how lucky Lady Luck had given a smack on the cheek. On December 14th we were officially being passed out of training and with a goodwill spirit, we were to have two weeks' leave instead of the usual seven days as was customary for the completion of training.

With the last remaining week or so, we all turned our minds to writing home with the good news as well as giving our families details of the rail services. Letters came back full of joy and pleasure. I'm not sure who was more excited, our folks or we lads. But what a tremendous boost to our egos. We were going home for Christmas! The Christmas of 1943.

We were off on shore leave as often as we could, painting the town red, as the saying goes. Enjoying ourselves as best we could, of course at the back of our minds was the ever presence of war. Back at barracks, a cloud began to form over our breezy feelings. The very day before we were to leave for home, orders came through to tell us we were to muster at 0800 hours at the drill shed, dressed in overalls, tin hat and a stout pair of boots. The final test of skill had arrived. We were to be pulled through the camp's notorious assault course, where we had to swim fully-clothed, jump trenches, bayonet dummy enemies, fire beneath barbed wire fences, around gate posts, bridges, hedges, and the sudden appearance of the ghastly mud bath.

If we dared think of a sunny day to go through our paces, we were very sadly disheartened. The rain just poured down, and what made it worse was the fact that the chief petty officer in charge of the evil goings-on piped up to say the day was just right to go mud paddling. Some of the lads were wide-eyed at that thought. I had to smile a little. After all, we were going home very soon. Needless to say, the rain continued to fall in sheets. There we were, poorly clad in overalls, singlet and shorts. Already soaked to the skin, and a smiling officer to boot! Rifles and all our equipment were sodden and heavy. Off we trotted. It was easy over the concrete roads, but we did eventually hit the mud and slime. I imagined that all this was well planned with the powers-to-be. Rifle firing didn't go down too well because the barrels were clogged with the good old mud. There was no time for complaining. I would have a job anyway because I got a mouth full of mud. I caught a glance of my mate, Phil, as he hit the mud. Other lads were not doing so good either, but light-hearted, we carried on. Time to reach the river and I must say it didn't look too friendly, but in we had to plunge, and being up to our waists in water made a hard job of trying to keep afloat. With a muddy face, I had to smile as a few of the lads overbalanced and disappeared in the not-too-friendly swirl. Other lads were more fortunate and managed to keep their heads above water. I was one of these few, but instead of water, I was covered with thick mud from head to toe. Needless to say, I think every one of us really enjoyed the fun and the ducking. Why not? There was a smashing hot shower after it and a good night's sleep was very well-deserved. Sleep was wonderful and I knew on the morrow our course at HMS *Raleigh* would come to an end.

All we had to do now was to pack our kit and lash up our hammocks — we were experts at this after long, long practice. The truth of the matter was we were really sleeping in bunks at the camp, but we had to get the practice with the hammocks, which by the way, brought many funny goings-on while we did practice. Slinging the hammocks came easy; getting into the hammocks, one would say, was more of a disaster. The moment you tried to get into the hammock on one side, the swing got you flying out the other side. But all this was overcome with time, and so it was. There were grim-looking faces at the thought of getting into the water with and without life jackets. There was many a tummy filled with an extra supply of water at that time. What some of the lads went through would fill a book of comic jokes. One lad took the prize for being the silly duffer — he must have thought he was a cat because he tried in vain to crawl up the side of the pool in desperation. He was yanked out of the water post-haste and ordered to get back into the water and try lifesaving exercises again and again. He was a good sport and got the drill down to a fine art. I thank the Lord I was a keen swimmer, having spent a lot of time at the local pool in my home town of Pontypool.

After the pool routine, most of us had sore arms and legs, but life must go on, as they say — we had orders to muster to. The challenge was at the gymnasium. The gym was not too inviting I must say, it stood there ready to do justice to a lot of misfits. Wooden monster and dangling ropes. No time to stand and heavy of heart. There were ropes to climb and conquer. There were wooden horses to straddle while trying not to damage any vital parts. There were bikes and dumbbells putting us dumbbells to shame, but we got through the lot with flying colours. We left the gym feeling alive and fresh, but we were not fresh enough to be smelling like roses, not to mention the bruises we had mustered in places that are not seen too often. In the end, we knew we had overstayed our welcome and left the camp as young men who were growing up very fast.

We left HMS *Raleigh* for the last time as colours was about to sound, and that would be the last time we would hear it. We felt a little glum at leaving new mates. Transport was already lined up on the driveway and it took us no time at all to get settled on the coaches. After the cheers from pals from camp who were seeing us off and the waving of hands, we were at last on our way to the station at Plymouth, and with kit bags already packed and stacked on the railway platform, we waited for the train to arrive. It would be taking us away to our Christmas freedom as long as it would last. The waiting on the platform seemed to be taking forever, but, at last we were away.

NORTH SEA COMMAND

My leave began in a rush. I had quite a lot of people to see. After greetings and hugs and kisses, the conversation would start with the question of how long will my leave would last. The question I dreaded was, did I expect to return to the Navy? I was glad to catch up with my school pal, Roy. He was not in the forces at that time but still working at his old job in Pontnewynydd. He was to enlist after the Christmas holidays. But in the meantime, both of us painted our small market town red. We took to the dance hall and caught up with many an old girlfriend. We got to parties and had great walks through the countryside, when the weather was kind to us that is. About a week into my leave, I happened to be at a Saturday night dance and there I met a girl I had known for a while before the Navy took me off. This was Edna, the girl I really took a fancy to, and whilst on leave, we saw a lot of each other. I was a frequent visitor to her home, and I did enjoy her parents' company as well.

Christmas Day came and went. With it, of course, came much fun and laughter, wine and song. Sometimes a tear or two crept in. I was not lucky enough to spend the New Year at home because my leave came to an end just a few days before. After the parting of such sweet sorrow, I wended my way to the railway station. As I sat waiting for the train, I thought of the first time I had left home for the Navy. That parting lasted just three months. Now that I was away again, it would be much longer than three months.

On the way back to Plymouth, the train picked up a number of the lads from the camp, but it was not until we had arrived at Plymouth that I caught up with two of my best mates, Dave and Phil. There sure was a lot of talk about with whom did they meet and where did they go and how many girls did they kiss. What a life! We eventually found our way to the waiting transport and off we went to the barracks, known to the township as HMS *Drake*. The building looked sinister and forlorn with its high walls and huge gates, and of course the many patrols everywhere. The Officer of the Watch was at this post looking equally as sinister as the Quarterdeck where he stood giving all of us the once-over. We got the salute routine down to a fine art. One or two of the lads apparently missed out on their salute because the Officer of the Watch yelled to the offenders asking them if they were half asleep, and if so, they should turn-about-face, come back and salute and don't forget to do it AT THE DOUBLE. The rest of us took this warning in good spirits and at last moved forward.

We did enter HMS *Drake* with a feeling of great expectation and as we passed right through the gates and heard them shut again behind us, somehow the glory of entry seemed to be slightly dimmed. I heard one lad, close behind me, remark that this was the end of freedom. As we moved further into the barracks, we began to get used to the feeling of being surrounded by high walls and many armed guards. Really, the place was like a small town. It appeared we would not want for anything. But later, we were always glad to get out of the place for awhile, and with maybe only a short stay before getting a ship, things were not too bad. Lo and behold! Suddenly there was much talk about some of us being drafted to Scapa Flow, right up there in the Orkney Islands. Not only that, the name of the ship was on everyone's lips — the aircraft carrier, *Furious*. It was not going to be a battleship. It was not going to be a destroyer or a smaller ship. We comprehended that it all might be a bluff on someone's part and so the gossip continued to spread throughout the barracks. No concrete development was issued in our search for news. Mum was the word! We had to settle down as best we could and wait the long hours away. We all knew however, there would be some kind of ship. A ship we would be calling home for some time to come. As for myself, I was very eager to get on with my part of the war. Little did I think that would be very, very soon.

I had my good and bad piece of news as quick as you can wink. Dave and I were off to the *Furious*, but Phil was to remain in barracks. Here is where I got my good and bad news. The good news was that Dave was coming to the same ship as I was. But sorry to say, Phil was to be left behind in barracks. This was disappointing news indeed. We had all been such good pals and had been together ever since we first got ourselves into the Navy. It was bad luck indeed. As usual, we all took the news with a brave smile. Sadly, that was the last time I saw Phil, on that very cold December day. From our coach, we waved Phil goodbye as he disappeared from view. Little did I know that we would never meet again. My mind flooded forward a trillion years and I wondered, would it be possible to think we could meet at home somewhere? I had the idea of trying to look him up straight after the war. The coach suddenly gave a lurch, bringing me back to reality.

My mind quickly came back to the present — giving a sigh my mind turned to the six of us who were about to begin new adventure. There were six of us on our way to the blue seas yonder. Dave and I were together, and just as well because this trip was a long one. Our destination was way up north at a place named Thurso — almost at the tip of Scotland — two days and a night on the train. I never really knew if I enjoyed the trip or not, but conversation was never lacking. Eventually, Thurso got itself on our horizon and at once I thought a nice hot meal would be really appreciated. Naturally we were given meals on the train. Putting one's feet on firm ground again was indeed grand. The next stage of the journey was to be taken by steamer. Would you believe it? We had to pick a day when the weather was not too kind at all. There was a strong wind and the sea was at its roughest. My very first ship, and very small at that. The lads were no comfort as we went aboard. We knew very well the trip would be a rocky one — and rock it did! It did everything but turn over. Being a true-blue sailor, I'm glad to say the motion of the vessel did not bother me one bit, but looking at Dave's green face, I knew he had eaten too much at that last meal.

I took stock of the other lads and I knew poor Dave was not on his own in the seasick department. With a stout heart, we knew we had to keep our chins up even if it did mean a lot of chin stretching. Everyone got through their ordeal in true Navy fashion, but we were all glad to reach the calmer waters of the bay. It really was a godsend as we entered the bay. Inside the protection of the group of islands was truly welcome. The sea takes on a calmness that is great for suffering travellers, such as a group of sailors! Faces suddenly took on a new perspective, because gone was the rocking and pitching and turning and rolling. I smiled to myself as I thought how good it was to have peace at last. I felt some relief myself as the time came to leave the steamer. The next ship was going to be another sort of barracks which we had been used to. We were to be housed there until our ship would be willing to take us on board. It wasn't too bad on this old vessel; she was moored to the spot and never likely to ever move away again. The ship had done all the sea trips that had been expected of her and the name she bore was very becoming. She was the *Iron Duke*.

Dave and I still kept close together throughout our stay on the *Iron Duke*. Discipline of course was very naval, and the weather was none too kind, and by this time the old year had bowed its head and departed, making way for the new one. In the evening, Dave and I were happy to go up on the upper deck and play a game of peering through the gloom trying to spot our next ship as she was laying at anchor out there in the gathering wind and snowflakes. Our mysterious HMS *Furious* — but the game brought no results. In the end, we decided to let fate take its course and give us one hell of a surprise when we first set eyes on the *Furious*. Being up on deck was becoming a bit of a problem as the wind took on a much sharper tone of voice. Even the waters of the bay seemed to dance and boil. Below deck was the answer, and that is just where we went. Just in time to hear the loudspeaker give out its message. At last we were told some of us were being shipped to our respective postings.

Most of the lads were now leaving. Being true sailors, some of them delighted in shouting down the hatch, telling us they would meet ashore if we ever got a ship. To me, I got a blunt message telling me if I ever got a ship I should broadcast it to the fact that the ruddy war was already over. Bloody cheek! Of course, everything was in good fun and we did enjoy the true friendship of our mates-at-arms. At this point, Dave and I were left on our own. Had they forgotten us? Dave thought all wrong things by saying maybe they were going to send us back to where we came from, and he didn't mean jolly old England.

It seemed hours and hours since the other lads left the *Iron Duke*. Even I began to chew over the remarks Dave made. I can say we were both a bit fed up with the thought of our next ship slipping its moorings and leaving us both on the *Iron Duke* for the rest of the war. But as luck would have it, from out of the silence came the orders for ratings to the *Furious*, the boat was alongside. Did Dave and I jump? Did we ever! In no time at all we were both racing as fast as we could towards the gangway, and at the same time the sun burst through the clouds to greet us on our way. There they all were, the fleet in bathing sunshine. A sight I shall remember all the days of my life — as long as life would last that is. Dave and I had the same question on our minds. Which of all these ships was ours? I asked one of the boat's crew, could he point out the *Furious* for us? He gave a smile and told me, 'You can't see her from this point, kid. You'll have to wait 'til we get to the other side.' I silently asked myself, what's the other side? The next thing he told me almost blew my top off. He said in a very proud sounding voice that they keep all the carriers over there. Dave and I almost fell off our seats as we called out 'Carriers'. The crew member gave a laugh and asked us, didn't we know we were part of the crew of *Furious*? Then he added that the *Furious* was a famous aircraft carrier and that we should be very proud to become part of her crew. She's in and out of harbour all the while, he added with relish. Not much of the enemy gets past the old warrior. We both sat there a little spellbound and we could hardly contain ourselves as we moved off. A short while after we took off, one of the other crew began to tell us that the *Furious* was a converted carrier. She had no funnels, but had smoke ducts right at the stern. You might find her a bit different from the more modern carriers, but believe me boys, she can hold her own amongst the rest of 'em. As we pushed on, I turned my head and watched the *Iron Duke* fade out of sight. A few minutes later, the sun began to take on watery effect. I noticed more and more grey clouds taking over from the small patch of blue. Wouldn't you know it! The sea began to get more restless; trust us to hit a storm before we could be safe and sound aboard our very own carrier. The rising wind did us no favour as it tipped cold water over the boat, not to mention icy seawater in our faces and down our necks. Dave stated the obvious by saying, we sure can pick a nice day for a boat ride.

The worst was yet to come.

Just a few minutes after the wind decided to take hold, the first flakes of snow fell. Just a gentle flutter at first, then thicker and faster until the flakes began to blind us all. Not only looking like snowmen, we were simply frozen to the marrow. Nothing could be seen, but the sudden hollow and lonesome sounds of the foghorns could he heard through the blizzard. It seemed a lifetime before the snow eased, the wind took a little longer to give up its strength to give us time to look around us. At least the crew knew where they were heading. Our long-awaited search for the *Furious* had come to an end because there she was, just ahead. We said nothing as we got closer. Dave and I glanced at each other but said nothing, the sight before us told the story. Such a huge ship! Much longer than any of the other ships, and lo and behold, there were really no funnels. We watched the smoke rising from aft of the ship. The flight deck had that strange look about it. First impressions they say, are always important. My impression wanted me to smile a little. I should not say *Furious* looked somehow funny, it was more like being overwhelmed. But with doubts and fancy aside, we were glad to get aboard.

It did not take us long to get used to the ship. As for myself, I was very glad we had all arrived in one piece. Our first salute as we climbed aboard put a lump in my throat. We waited for our kit bags to come aboard and then we were taken below decks to get our names along those of the ship's company. How important that sounded! I had the sudden feeling of being warm and comfortable as we went through the formalities. The rest of the day was spent getting used to our surroundings. Later, we were told to be outside the Master-at-Arms office at 0830 the next morning. At last we were on our very own ship. Luck was on our side as Dave and I were put on the same duty watches. Also, we were assigned to the same Action and Cruising Stations. I knew *Furious* was going to be my lucky ship. We were drilled about the whereabouts of the rest of the fleet and the times when we were likely to set out to sea. How long we were going to stay in Scapa Flow was the very burning question.

Finding out about the ship's history was like unwrapping the pages of history itself. *Furious* was one of the ships to traffic planes on and off her flight deck. She had survived the perils of the First World War and was in the front line in this present conflict. She had not long returned from America where we were told the people there gave the boys the time of their lives. It was a shame how we had missed that trip, but as they say, what you don't have you don't miss. It did not take long to gain some knowledge of our future undertakings. The buzz was a run through the North Sea, the Arctic region, the Russian conveys, and last but not least, the thrills and excitement with sights I shall never forget. At last, we were really a part of the Home Fleet, and the North Sea Command.

TO THE FJORDS OF NORWAY

Our lives aboard *Furious* became complete in no time at all. Dave and I became known as forecastle men and very recent landlubbers — a name we were very keen to dismiss. We were busy learning the jobs of raw recruits, this important job and the not-so-important duties becoming to an ordinary seaman. I enjoyed the routine of getting used to Navy life. I was a little surprised at the thought of being allowed shore leave there in Scapa Flow. There was no need to go sightseeing because there was nothing to see for miles. If you were fond of a study of rocks, that might be paradise for some folk. As for trees, you might as well forget it. But still, being on strange ground was a pleasure in itself. Of course, when it isn't raining you can expect it to snow. One bright aspect was the island did have a cinema — and we had one on board and good times were had through this medium. I left going ashore to the lads who had leg stretching to do. But through the cruel winter months all the lads seemed to take things in good part. Even the routine of prayers each morning seemed quite normal and Stand Easy at 10.30 each morning was something to look forward to. Lunch at midday became a favourite habit when not on duty. Part of ship duty came to an end at 1600 hours. All this was in harbour routine. At sea, the whole ship's company went on sea watches. So much time on watch, so much time off watch. As we were in harbour, most activities on board stopped at 1600 hours. Of course, there were always   watch keepers doing duties, and in those duties everyone was involved. However, time did not stand still on board the *Furious*, but both Dave and I sailed through the times and were quite ready for the happening to come.

Winter was at its pitch when one day orders came through from the Captain's Office. The orders were for painting the ship. All sorts of visions sprang to mind. Painting ship! How, where and when? Over the side was my first reaction that was not far from the truth, as a matter of fact, I hit the bull's-eye. In the tropics, it might have been really good. Out there in Father Christmas land I really had doubts. I got caught in the struggle to see who was going to get the best spots to paint. Somehow, I knew the best patches would be allotted to long term ratings. I knew our part of the ship was the bows. The bows were on the urgent list and so it was. The weather was none too grand as the work got under way. The painting was to be done in stages, a fancy name for the dull colours that were to come, I thought. We took our turns at popping over the side of the ship in our stages. Getting over the side of the ship could very well cause a problem to some lads who were not too keen on heights. The method was to drop planks on ropes and pulleys, and then the real meaning of stages became clear — the stages were no other than the planks we were to sit on while painting the sides of the ship. Glory be! I murmured under my breath followed by an understanding smile. Lowering ourselves as each section was completed. This also was a problem for one and all. It was imperative that we lowered the planks together at the same time. Two to a plank saw enough to make that perfect drop. Did it become perfect every time? I don't think I shall go into that! However, we did drop in stages as the painting was completed, that is until we came to the water's edge or rather to the water line, from where we used the boat's long tom brushes, as these had very long handles. Needless to say, we took all this in great fun — but being covered in paint was another matter. If the Captain only knew how much paint we wore. A question not to be answered! We did wear overalls so that was a blessing. However, one extremely cold morning as we got to the next patch close to the water line, there were even a few patches of blue sky to be seen. My mate on the other side of our plank asked, 'What's happened to the weather?' Then I, too, remarked how mild and calm it felt. We enjoyed this bit of luxury for a short while until I happened to glance up at the sky, and there, coming at us was the darkest cloud bank I had ever seen. I yelled to my mate to remind him that we were enjoying the calm before the storm. My mate yelled back that we should get the hell out of there. At that very moment a voice called down to us from the upper deck to tell us to get up on deck and be mighty quick because there was a blizzard headed straight for us. We had no time to gather our thoughts. We had no time to manoeuvre ourselves, and to make matters worse, the same voice yelled to tell us it would not be very nice to get covered in those nice white snow feathers. Indeed, we had no chance of getting back on deck before the storm hit us. So, there we were as the blizzard hit us, and hit us hard it did. The snow seemed to fall in sheets and the wind grew very savage and rocked us like a rocking horse. There was no need to tell my mate to hang on like grim death, one false move and we were going to take a midwinter swim. It was too dangerous to try climbing up to the deck, the swinging ropes were enough to tell us to continue hanging on. We could not see each other through the blinding snow. Through the turmoil of the storm I heard shouting and yelling like blue murder. Orders were being screamed out to get the bloody boat over the side before those two bastards meet up with Neptune and his gang. I gave a very nervous laugh, but did not intend to meet up with the old man of the deep just yet, and the fact that the snow was already inches deep on our overalls didn't improve matters much. More voices bellowed through the snow to hurry up with the boats before the lads are washed out to sea. That announcement we could do without as we did a kind of trapeze act on the lurching planks. Thoughts of a warm hammock passed through my very tired brain as we waited what seemed like weeks to get rescued. Then, just out of the blue shall we say, the rotten storm passed on; we stopped dancing and our blistered hands felt like fire itself, but all we got for our savage misadventure was lots of laughter from the decks above. I heard someone shout that there were two snowmen coming aboard, and aboard we did come at last to be taken below decks and wrapped mercifully in lots of warm blankets.

The topic of conversation for a while was the incident of the hanging snowmen. For a few days we got a ribbing, but behind the jokes I knew there had been grave fears for us, and I was glad for the hidden good humour of one and all. But I thought to myself that when the next snow storm hit us, I hoped to be well and truly safe below decks. I should have known better; there would be plenty of storms while we were out at sea, and there was a beauty of a storm one day when Dave and I were on watch together. We had the morning watch from midnight until four in the morning on number one gun in the bows of the ship. Dave was lucky to have missed my painting storm, but this one he had no way of missing, but that story will have to come a little later on.

Anyway, at last, the painting of the ship was completed. All nice and clean looking. *Furious* was ready for all comers, come hell or high waters. Looking nice and clean as I put it, didn't last too long where the *Furious* was concerned. The latest buzz began to circle around the ship. At last, we were off to Norway. Dave said he heard the news from outside the galley. One of the older seamen mentioned the ship would head out to join the Russian convoy. Someone else would say they heard Jimmy telling Flags to translate all this gossip. Translate would be the right word to explain that Jimmy really meant the First Lieutenant and Flags is meant to be the Flag Officer in charge of signals. We shall find more words that need explaining as we go along, but those bridges are best used as we cross them.

The buzzes continued to get around the ship. Then suddenly, one day the Captain put all speculation to rest. The news came over the loudspeakers that evening. I saw Dave just before the news, he had just come off duty aft or stern as some would have it. Dave remarked that it sounded as if we were about to leave Scapa Flow at last. The whole ship's crew was bent on waiting for the broadcast. I took a turn up on deck to get a little fresh air — and that is what I got alright. It was bitterly cold, and the wind remained a little mischievous, but up on deck I met happy-go-lucky Strippy. He was really a man who could wipe away all your troubles with his broad Scotch accent. Strippy was on the same gun as Dave and I were on at action stations. Strippy was our range finder and he really did know how to handle that job. He was the one who coached me to become an able seaman, what giddy height that was! We got to talking about all the chatter about the pending run. He said it was best left to the Captain's broadcast. We had been talking for a good half an hour when suddenly the Quarter Master came along doing his rounds and he told us to beat it below decks if we wanted to hear the Captain's broadcast, and it did not take us long to do just that. We were just in time to hear him as he said, 'This is the Captain speaking,' and he went on to tell us all about our forthcoming orders. The buzz was more or less correct. We were given orders to make our way north. Time permitting, we were to assist on the Russian Convey. However, our main objective was to hunt out and find the dreaded, one and only ship, the Admiral Von *Tirpitz*. The German battleship of notorious fame.

This ship was the deadly menace that waited in the northern regions, hindering our shipping. The *Tirpitz* dealt deadly blows to our merchant Navy ships and the orders were to hunt out and destroy this ugly monster at all costs. The *Tirpitz* was hiding out in the fiords of Norway and it was our job to wait for her until she came out of hiding on one of her blistering attacks on our convoys. We all knew from the very first that it was going to be a cat-and-mouse game. The thoughts of the weather being against us and being at the mercy of the Arctic sea, made me realise that it was going to be very cold and I would imagine, unbearable to watchmen on upper deck duties. The Captain reminded all of us that we must — and will — complete our mission to the best of our ability. Reading between the lines, we knew the onslaught would commence at once. Also, to await further orders. In the meantime, we were to collect warm clothing from the storeroom.

Everyone was in a state of excitement. Writing home with the good news was of course out of the question. We all knew letters to our loved ones would not be so frequent, and in no way could we give them any hints of our mission. It sounded like the hand of doom had descended upon us. War was war, and we had to take fate as it was handed out to us. I imagine the ship's censor would be very busy keeping news home under strict security. Anyone trying to give our whereabouts away would be in very deep trouble. The least slip of news could mean the cause of many men's lives. The very thought of us having to abandon ship was too horrible to imagine. Survival in the mid-Arctic would be impossible. It had been drummed into us about the consequences of being dumped at sea. Icy water would freeze a body in a minute. Thick, burning oil on open flesh. Long hair, a sure way of blinding you. All this was planted firmly in the brain. Through all our thoughts and letter writing, the Captain and his officers were planning our secret hunt of Norway.

At least tension was a great deal slackened with the fun we had down at the storeroom. Naturally there were many different shapes and sizes to consider, but being a little fusspot was not to the Navy conditions. For instance, shorty Jenkins was blessed with a duffle coat that could have been a dressing gown, while lofty Adams could do nothing with a duffle coat way above his knees. I saw Dave being decked out with his warm clothing fitting him to a tee. As for myself, the laws of body-making also favoured my desires. The going was good on the whole. There was no one who had to grumble to anyone who cared to listen. The main thing was that we did have the right clothing for the trip we were to embark on. The thought of these items not being allotted to us would not be worth talking about. I did witness some other misfits, but good humour was the order of the day. We were about to take on the challenges of a lifetime. Nothing could dim our stout hearts above that. I didn't wish the *Tirpitz* God's speed except to wish her a trip to the bottom of the sea.

THE ADMIRAL VON TIRPITZ

There was much that had to be done before we actually made our move. At least the warm clothing was well underway. We could be away weeks or even months on the tail of the *Tirpitz*. All the warm clothing we needed would be welcomed. Time seemed to stand still as we waited for the time to depart. We were just completing our ablutions when the orders were given to up anchor and aweigh. There was a rush to finish dressing and getting as quick as we could to our stations. During the dashing about, I bumped into another pal named Eddie, and whilst we were aboard, we became quite good mates. Eddie, Dave and I remained together as we watched Scapa Flow slip slowly away out of sight. Many thoughts passed through my mind as we slowly made our way clear of the islands. All watch keepers were on their afternoon duties. They would be at their posts until 1600 hours. Then the change to the first dog watch from 1600 to 1800 hours. The last dog watch coming from 1800 to 2000 hours. Different ratings for different watches and then came the first watch 2000 to 2400 hours followed by middle watch 2400 to 0400 hours. Morning watch was a delight for some ratings with a chance to see a new day arriving. The forenoon watch was just what it sounded like, and so the whole routine started off again.

Within a few hours, we had lost all sight of land. Only sea and sky to match our view. It was not exactly calm waters we were sailing through because there was a heavy swell we managed to run into, and the further we got from Scapa, the worse the swell became. I was a little surprised to be feeling alright, just like an old salt, shall we say? But if I thought that joy was going to last, I was going to be very much mistaken.

Anyway, life on board was as normal as it could possibly be. I completed my watch on number one gun right up there in the bows of the ship, and as usual got lashings of spray. Just to make my watch more interesting, the occasional storm made itself felt. Somehow, however, I really sensed the scene was set for real drama. For days we sailed on without seeing any sight of land but I suppose that was to be expected. Having to put up with the not-too-friendly weather seemed to come as a natural course of events. Off duty, we had the chance of sleep, that is when you get used to the hum of the aircraft on the flight deck and numerous noises from the hangers below decks. The *Furious* boasted two hangers, of course, the temperature was much more comfortable that the swirling weather up on deck.

Good luck to the lads who were assigned to duty below decks. I had my misgivings about duties close to the planes. I think it must have been the presence of the fumes that were obvious to one and all, even with the wind, the rain and snow I really felt more at home for some reason other than the noise and fumes. On duty watch, on the gun there was a bit of fun between the eight of us that manned it. I was the loader while Dave was on ammunitions, but the important post when not in action was the guy on the headphones. Someone had to man the phones at all times, so we all took turns at this post. We might do an hour each and then give our ears a rest, and in the meantime we were not too far away from the gun. There was always the luxury of reading a book, or as we might say, glaring at all the pictures therein. I'm glad to say we were all sweet tempered and if there were funny things happening around the ship you could bet we made the most of savouring it. Some lads would be reminiscent of their going on during blind dates, some tall tales, who told them, have to be lodged to the imagination. One of the older ratings took the prize for very close mishaps. Apparently his one-off date in America had more evenings out on her mind. She took a real shine to this innocent lad and she said he would be a wonderful father for her four nippers. It took him quite some time to unleash himself from that memory. But anyway, only roars of laughter heralded that rosy tale. Lots of funny stories sweeping around the gun site and anything was better than the pressure of standing around in a gloomy world of dark sky and grey seas.

The days passed by without a sign of combat, or the slightest sign of danger. Then suddenly, one very black and dismal afternoon when most of the lads were having the daily smoko, over the horizon came the signs of smoke. Was this something to change our way of life? I wondered.

After all, it could mean we were at last catching up with the Russian Convey. As regards to any action with the enemy, we might as well be laying in our beds fast asleep. We were, however, content to escort quite a number of conveys without undue danger to the ships. Then suddenly, one stormy day when all seemed peaceful and serene, there was an urgent call to Action

Station. Submarines were sighted too close for comfort. There had been several attempts at torpedo attacks on vessels on the fringes of the convoy. Then, grim orders for depth charges to be dropped. The bastard Germans got one of our smaller carriers and instantly, the unlucky vessel began to list. It was unbelievable to stare across the water and see destruction so swift and evil. They must have been ordered to abandon ship because through tears of blinding fury I watched the imperative that we keep a cool head. Blasting off the guns without direct orders was out of the question. But God had mercy, that particular carrier did not sink and hopefully the ship's crew were saved. In the meantime, I glanced around at the faces of our gun's crew. I saw determination there. Dave gave me a wink. I winked back — we would survive. We were glad of the news that the stricken carrier could limp back to Scapa under her own steam, to be patched up and back on duty, ready for action again.

At last we knew we had to be ready for any kind of action and it was always wise to keep one hand on your life jacket. God only knew when or if your number was up. It had been drummed into us about sub attacks. The crew of those deadly man-eaters were very cunning indeed. These subs would turn up anywhere and at any time of night or day. They often tailed us on these arctic runs, but somehow they could not get near enough to cause our ship damage. The floating mines were an extreme menace to any ship afloat. We were all very diligent in these matters. Foggy days proved to be very dangerous as visibility was very poor, and more than once we took a few near misses. Thank God for the men with the sharpest eyes. These lookouts were trained to perfection. This was a serious command for the Royal Marines on board. These men would be posted about the ship looking for floating debris of any kind. With rifles at the ready, they were expert marksmen, fancy shooting you would not believe. Now and again there would be a gigantic explosion and one more terror of the deep would be destroyed. Cheers all round followed such success. Then, back to the never-ending search. I was truly amazed at the cunning way these mines were laid, stretched out to destroy shipping of any size. If a vessel hit one of these spikes it would be catastrophic. I remember that listed carrier and was not ashamed to give a very cold shiver. Everyone on board was very thankful for the powers of our marines. It somehow reminded me of the rifle range as the marines did their expert jobs, but out there in the very cold climate everything was so real. Hitting such a small object in the vast expanse of ocean was a wonder beyond imagination.

My mind wandering back to the dreaded *Tirpitz* was no fun indeed. Impracticable, just as the restless ocean. Duty was foremost on everyone's mind and we vowed to chase the *Tirpitz* to the end of the earth if necessary. The thought of seeing this fight to the end was second nature to every man on board.

Suddenly, out of the blue, the whole fleet seemed to stand still. I thought my eyes were playing tricks on me. A few of us were on deck watching over the ships but none of the other ratings seemed to be conscious of the event I thought I saw. But thank goodness the truth dawned on the others. We were altering course. Suddenly, there was reaction about the whole ship. I noticed there was lots of activity. There must have been a nest of subs close at hand. I swept the ocean with my ears and eyes, but everything seemed quiet. I was expecting all sorts of urgent commands from the bridge. I even had the thought that a massive storm was about to hit us. The lads around appeared tense as we waited for some sort of action from the bridge. The motion of the ship changed and one of the ratings close by spoke in a very sarcastic whisper, saying that maybe we were making a run for it. I stared at him for a moment with a glare of anger in my eyes. I could have easily picked him up and thrown him overboard, but I noticed he was much heavier than I was. Lifting him over the side would be something of a problem. I did the next best thing by giving him a sharp dig in the ribs. He laughed and told me he was only joking. Someone else suddenly called out to say we were really altering course. My mate with the sore ribs yelled, 'Bloody hell, don't tell me we are really making a run for it?'

We did alter course, but it was not only *Furious* that changed directions. Within a few minutes, more of the fleet followed suit and it was not long before we had left the convoy far behind. Sailing with us then were other carriers, one or two battleships and destroyers. Dotted about were cruisers keeping in close contact with the others in the fleet.

We knew then that something important was about to happen. We were not wrong. The *Tirpitz* had been sighted trying to leave her den. That was the news we had all been waiting for. We all hoped the *Tirpitz* had made one little slip too many. *Furious* came alive with preparations for the pending attack. The watch was ordered to be ready at any moment. Our guns were always at the ready. The planes were fuelled for the coming onslaught. Ammunition for the cannons and the other types of weapons. Everything checked and again rechecked. The first squadron of planes were standing by. Then came the waiting.

Waiting became unbearable. A real distraction from boredom was the fact we could watch the wonder of the northern lights. This was a sight worth its very weight in gold. In the middle of terrible war, such a sight was most welcome. The sky became a mass of moving lights. You become fascinated and spellbound watching this creation of nature. These masses of lights running across the sky somehow made me think of Guy Fawkes Night. One great scene, other than the lights, came to us as we neared the Norwegian coast. The rocky cliffs were a maze of colour. The snow-capped hills were a thrilling sight. For a moment, the thoughts of war were a million miles away. It was impossible to even try counting the colours that hung there, and with a background of greyish-red clouds and the dense green of the sea, it was fantasy in itself. How could anyone imagine amongst all this beauty, there was lurking swift and sudden death? How could there be the suffering of the Norwegian people? How long I watched this magnificent spectacle I hate to think, because all around me was the thought of pending battle. The roar of the plane's engines brought me back to reality with a thump. The planes were off to try to force the *Tirpitz* to make a run for it. The bombs would be enough to cause great damage if our lads were lucky enough to hit their target. One of the main factors for success was a clear sky. At that moment, the planes' departure was rather dubious. We watched the planes take off with our fingers crossed and saw them disappear in the distance. Now the silence of waiting took over the whole ship. Great expectations for our pilots was evident on every man's face. Would this first hop be a hit on the *Tirpitz*? It seemed a million years later when one plane was sighted coming out of the mist. We all took our places to watch the spectacle. We watched them circle and land on the flight deck one after the other. Not a word was uttered as we waited for news from the Captain. The news came through with joyful cheers. The mission had been successful. The mighty terror of the deep had been hit. There had been attack after attack. Direct hits had been recorded on the ship and very close around it. Other shipping had been hit also. The whole mission had been a victory for our pilots. How many direct hits were obvious with the amount of damage reported. The *Tirpitz* was seen to be listing. The planes had done their duty and we were very pleased with the operation. The *Tirpitz* had really been pounded until the vessel seemed masked in gunfire. When we ran out of ammunition, it was time for our planes to return to the ship.

However, the ship was moored in very tricky surrounding in the fiord. Consequently, our pilots were not able to get as close to the ship as they would have liked. However, the most important news was the *Tirpitz* at last had been hit and, we hope, unable to leave the shelter of her haven. If luck continued to be with us, a return mission would finish the *Tirpitz* once and for all. We had to make a return trip to Scapa for refuelling. We made that dash for our destination in good speed.

The news of the attack brought headlines to the newspapers, which does not happen too often. But this time, this news was great news. We entered Scapa with cheers and great joyful shouts of welcome from the ships that lined up for our entering harbour. In a matter of hours, we received orders to weigh anchor and set a course for Scotland. But first, we were to stream around the fleet and receive the victory salutes from each ship as we steamed out of Scapa.

This was one of the most thrilling times of my life. Standing there on the upper deck and enjoying the Navy way of saying thanks for the proud and good work done. And to top everything off, the Admiral was in the bows of his ship cheering with the rest of his men. Not until we were past the last ship did the cheering stop. With deep regrets, we made speed for the port of Rosyth in Scotland.

We were lucky enough to get some very pleasing news later that evening, a spot of news that would keep us writing home for days. The ship's company had been granted a short leave. The reason was a saucy one. The ship was to have her bottom scraped and of course cleaned. The grime collected there was slowing up the ship's speed. This was a job for the dry dock. I think we all were very thankful for the *Furious* to have a dirty bottom! Mercifully, the weather was much milder in Scotland. In no time at all, we were snuggled in dry dock. Needless to say, most of the ship's crew were very busy indeed preparing for the short leave. Dave and Eddie were on leave with me. Some lads were to take leave a few days later.

In no time at all, we were off to the railway station and eventually on board the train, not to mention we were all as happy as we could be — singing and making merry. Why not indeed? We were bound for home.

The few days we had at home were very good. Eddie lived fairly close to me, so he came over to my place and we left for the station together. That last day we just sat at home and spoke of the things we did while we were at home with our families. We sat on the seat at the station in rather a glum mood until the train arrived to carry us off back to Scotland. We did not see very much of Dave during the rest of our stay in Scotland. But Eddie and I did what we could to have a fairly good time. Dances were always welcomed, and the picture shows passed the time away nicely. Outside, there was plenty to see; the people were very kind to us and so the time went by until all the ship's crew were aboard and waiting for the orders to leave port. The necessary work on the ship was carried out. I'm glad to say the ship now had a very clean bottom. The dry dock became part of the sea again and so we were ready to depart.

We slipped silently and smoothly out to the open sea to return to our Arctic mission — a mission in quest of the much-spoken Admiral *Tirpitz*. Our ship had become quite famous because of the very successful raid of a short while ago. We wasted no time in heading due north. It was good meeting up with Dave again, and in no time at all, long conversations were the orders of the day. There was a lot of catching up to do. Each one's holiday was best remembered in sweet dreams and reminiscence. We were that happy to be going home. I think even if it snowed until the cows came home, nothing was going to spoil this leave. Dave thought how lucky we had been to be part of such a battle. The *Tirpitz* was to be embedded in our minds forever. Eddie remarked how he would never forget the long waiting for our planes to return. For a while, we sat back and watched the scene outside the carriage slip away. I remembered the sudden sad faces on both Dave and Eddie.

Now, looking out over the cold ocean, even our short stay at home seemed miles and miles away. I suddenly made a point of stirring up the fire by asking Eddie if he had been making plans to get married at home. He almost fell over the rail and gave me a dig in the ribs. Eddie put a spoke in my wheel by asking if it was me who was planning to wed. They both knew I had a girlfriend I was very keen on, and they were about to play on that as far as they could go. I said the first thing that came into my head by telling them that all we did was drink iced cider in the Clarence Hotel. Our daydreaming came to a swift end as an order came through to tell us warm clothing was about to be distributed. Amid the scurry of collecting said warm gear, the usual tales of shore leave activities boiled over in the crew's conversations. I laughed at what Eddie had said about me. Lads were asking each other if they had got themselves married when on leave. Dave suddenly remembered how once on the mess deck he had caught me looking at a picture of my said-girlfriend. He brought that matter up by saying, 'Lover-boy Rogers might be on the way to the altar, lads.' I returned a swift gift to the ribs of Dave and wished to him that he would be getting his. A good job most of us have a thick skin with all the chatter going around. It was no good being high and mighty around these lads. That would be excuse for long-lasting ribbing. The same old routine followed with the misfits and funny sayings. I think life would become very dull if a bit of tomfoolery never existed.

Between the ribbing and letter writing, we sailed on to more glory. Once again, the cold snowy wastes surrounded us in the Arctic Sea. But at least the winter was at last showing signs of giving way to better conditions. Instead of semi-light we would be enjoying the midnight sun.

As we washed through this restless sea, the date of our next encounter came through. Our target was not able to venture for any distance. Our planes took off and made a beeline for their target and again the raids were successful. There had been dense smoke screens around the damaged ship, but determination on the part of our pilots proved no match. The *Tirpitz* was left to the mercy of the sea. We sailed up and down along the coast but there was no sign of hostility from the enemy. They were a cunning lot because they knew if they began firing this would give their positions away, which meant of course we could easily have blasted them to hell. In the meantime, we spent a few days escorting shipping bound for the Russian zone. This was a usual practice, and within a week we expected to find the *Tirpitz* under water. But when our bombers took off to circle the appointed region, they were to meet with a great surprise. The planes flew over the ridges and coves but through the gloom they found that the *Tirpitz* had vanished. She could not have sunk out of sight because the water was not deep enough to cover her completely. One conclusion was evident: the *Tirpitz* had been towed away.

This was no news for the whole ship's company. Every last man on board knew this was going to take a lot of searching. Could we dare hope to discover the *Tirpitz* hiding away amongst the many coves and hideaways along the coast? We knew the fiords were very tricky to search. There was much danger in the hillsides and cliffs that could contain air pockets to endanger flying too close. The only option was to cruise up and down the coast until we found out what had really happened to the *Tirpitz*.

In the hours of waiting, keeping on your toes proved a problem. At night-time there was something about the crisp air that made a person want to close their eyes and dream. Night watchmen had a hard time of it. Thinking up old songs brought some relief. Thoughts of home always gave the lads just a little warmth.

One night, it was my turn to take over the headphones. It was not the best night to be alone on the gun site on a cold night. The rest of the gun crew were hiding out of the cold wind amongst the piles of ammunition — they were contented. I settled down to stamping and blowing on my icy fingers, but at least I was lucky enough to have the weather fine. However, the sky did look somewhat a little too menacing, but so did everything else around me. It was peaceful enough, but my trouble had not started just then. I had not been on the phones ten minutes or so when something hit me full in the face. Did I give out a yell? Did I ever! My only thought, however, I imagined it to be a freak wave or something which needed a bit of explaining. But it was only a lump of ice, a hailstorm was in progress. Then, would you believe it, down came the snow as thick and as fast as the heavens would allow. I figured on being marooned again like the last time a month or so ago. I was completely covered with thick snow from head to toe. Thick layers on the deck, the railing, the lookout post. I thought to myself whether I should start singing Christmas carols or something. The wind took a turn in giving me havoc to fill my eyes with snow. It proved such a playful storm. I had about six inches of snow all around me. With a roar of laughter from one of the crew members, all he said was to the effect that I should not let snow cover the earphones. It's a good job he had come to relieve me, otherwise I might have been tempted to knock his block off. He hadn't finished with his clowning as he added that I should think of the other lads who had to come out in the cold and put ruddy snow-clad earphones on. I took control of my fake temper and moved off to the shelter of the ammo wind break when he added with all the sternness he could muster, 'Do you think it might snow on my watch, Ginger?' I answered back with an equal tone of voice to tell him to go play snowballs! I made myself as comfortable as I could with the other lads before helping myself to a cup of cocoa and crackers.

Sipping my cocoa, I thought about the lads in the planes. They had been out for quite a while. Looking for the ship would be no fun in this shocking weather. The news came back however to tell us there had been no sight of the *Tirpitz* anywhere. They might have hidden their prize battleship really well. The planes landed and took off again until one day, when a few of us were having a game on deck, enjoying the midnight sun, a sudden squall hit us. Before we could run for cover, the rain fell in sheets. It was one way of taking a shower up on deck. There really wasn't much difference between night and day. Even while on middle watch, midnight until four in the morning, you could be enjoying the midnight sun. So, such is life, they say.

It did take some getting used to, this strange weather, but used to it we had to be. However, it was strange to think that in the middle of the night you could be enjoying the fairly warm rays of the sun. At the moment though, there were a couple of seamen in need of some warm and dry clothing. Down to the showers and leg pulling as usual.

While in the shower, of course boys will be boys, and through the tomfoolery, the planes began to return to the ship with some great news. They had found the *Tirpitz*. But from where she was moored, a successful raid would not be possible. More damage to the *Tirpitz* was very unlikely. There were a few more attempts to destroy her just to make sure, but the job had to be left to the Air Force. The RAF with their long-distance bombers would have to carry on where the *Furious* had left off. There was much sadness in the heart of the *Furious* after the news. But as the Captain put it, *Furious* had done her best and we were to leave the rest of the operation to the pilots of the Royal Air Force. We knew the *Tirpitz* could not get clean away because of the damage our lads had inflicted on her. If the RAF could get in there fairly fast with no time lost, we might just win through after all. With a blood-red sunset and a million lights drifting through the sky, we left the coast of Norway.

On our way back to base, we called in at the Faroe Islands just off the Shetland Islands. The rocky hillsides did not appear at all welcoming. We entered the small bay in a heavy rainstorm. It looked as if it had never stormed before. The clouds were hanging very low over the island; what we could see was not very inviting at all. The rain continued through the night and the morning brought little change. The constant rain seemed to run in rivers across the flight deck. A high wind took its toll on everything. It lasted all that day, but when morning dawned, we found a completely new day. The scene had changed quite a lot. The sky was clear and very blue. My mind went back to Wales, where spring was about to raise its head along with my favourite flower, the daffodil. It was pleasing to see the island bathed in sunshine. A small town could be seen across the bay, and dotted about were little red and white houses. What a change a little sunshine can make. The next morning, we left for Scapa Flow. We arrived there also on the wings of spring.

HMAS HMS FURIOUS

It was rather nice to see Scapa Flow again. The whole scene was bathed in sunshine, but there was just a little snow still hanging around in patches. The weather was not as cold as it was the last time we were in port. When we departed a short while ago, the whole place was covered in a mantle of snow. We moored in our old bay just off the island. I wondered how long it would be before we enjoyed the midnight sun again. The whole crew was having a great rest and really enjoying it when news came through from the RAF reports. Their continuous attacks on the *Tirpitz* had at last finished her off. The great bombing had turned her over on her side. This was indeed great news. What luck to know that at least one great menace of the war was now just a bad memory. We were still busy with the convoys and waiting for orders to proceed. These duties were to last us right through the summer.

After every convoy duty, we were to return to Scapa Flow for a few days rest. However one trip was a little different. We were a part of a mission to turn over a battleship to the Russian Navy. The *Furious*, with other vessels, were to convoy our battleship into the Russian zone. The new crew were a mystery to us. We never saw them arrive to take over the battleship. Where they came from, not one of us knew. Nothing came from our Captain and nothing was relayed to us on any of the goings-on. But true to Navy fashion, as we passed the bows of their new ship, we would give them a cheer as they lined the ships decks. In return, each one of the crew gave us a salute. What a wonderful feeling to join such a friendly nation.

Shore time was spent with Dave and Eddie. The weather remained quite warm and a good time was had by all. Some of the evenings, the fleet took turns in giving the other ship a ball. There were WRENS on the island and everyone was glad of such entertainment. There were also WAAFS on the island, so there were plenty of partners and they too became part of the fun. Ashore was getting much better as the weeks turned into one month, then two. Spring began to turn into summer and still our convoy work went on. There had been talk of leave again — it had been quite a few months since those few days after our first attack on the *Tirpitz*. So we were again feeling ready for leave, but for the time being, we would be busy with the cleaning up of the ship, one more trip at sea and a few days again in the 'Flow' and up on the notice board came the names of the first lads to go on leave. Dave was to be among the first, Eddie and I the second.

It was a very long trip from Scapa to South Wales and remembering the first time we did it, months ago, I was thinking how tired everybody would be at the end of the trip. There was the trip by steamer to the far coastline of Scotland, then after that the two days and a night trip by train to our own hometowns. I was glad Eddie and I were to be together; it was much better having company. We had to get off the train at the same railway station, but Eddie was to go a little further up the valley than I. The first lads were to do their packing and be gone by the next morning. I went over to Dave, who by this time was in the "Watch keepers" mess. He had been put on the ship's switchboard and a good job, too. The other lad who was on it was a Welsh man by the name of Len; he was in the same mess as me and we got on well together. Dave was up to his neck in packing — socks and shoes everywhere. 'I don't think you will get them all in, Dave,' I said.

He replied with a smile, 'OK, Job's comforter, get cracking,' and with a roar of laughter I left him to his pushing and squeezing.

The morrow dawned none too quick for Dave, he had been restless all night and when it was time to be getting up, he had already been to the bathroom and waiting for breakfast. What a life for a fellow going on leave. But the time came and as each of us went off, we who were left on board lined the upper deck and said a few last cheerful words such as, 'Have a good time and don't drink the place dry. We have to go on leave too you know.' And when the last lot had gone, Eddie and I returned to our 'flats' below decks, we both had been taken from the upper deck and were given jobs down below. A flat is a part of the ship from water-tight door to water-tight door and our job was to keep these flats clean and tidy. Sometimes it was hard work scrubbing out, polishing all the brass work for the Captain's rounds each Saturday morning, but we got along with it alright, and when the Chief and our Officer in charge were not about, Eddie and I always had a good chat. Just like the poor hard-working women talking over the garden fence. But if any of these persons read these pages, I give my word, I am only kidding! This was to be done for another fourteen days until the other lads came back off leave. With four days there and back allowed for travelling, they would have ten days at home. Halfway of my leave, I thought. Now that the summer has arrived, I shall be able to go swimming at home in the pool, and I was also missing my dancing with Edna very much. We used to dance about four or five nights a week before I came into the Navy. That is a hard record to hold down, at Scapa I was lucky to get a dance once a month. But still, it will not be long now before I shall be home again, having the usual time of my life. We were all busy letting our folks know when to expect us and then we only had to carry on with our work, counting every hour and every minute.

Eddie and I went ashore a few times to the cinema, but not very often as we were more interested in getting things ready for our leave, washing out clothes and jerseys and all the necessary things one needs when going away for a while. When everything had been arranged, we discovered that in two days' time we were to set out on our trip to the coast and home once more. I did not know how many more leaves I would be having after this one, but between me and the gateposts, I was to have only one more leave and that was to be on "Embarkation Leave" but that was not to be found out by me for the next six months.

The next two days were very slow in passing. We continued on with our 'flats', wrote more letters at night, and took strolls on the flight deck, watching the soft summer sky changing from sunset into night. I often sat up there in the evening, the clouds would turn from white to bright red, then darker into almost black as the night advanced, covering everything with its mantle of velvet, not a light to be seen anywhere. The infernal blackout saw to all that, so when darkness really fell, I was off to the mess, writing or reading until the last night when I could not even concentrate. It was not only late, it was also the last evening before we were to go on leave so I did not wonder at all, I just slung my hammock and tried in vain to sleep. In the end, tiredness overcame me and I knew no more until the much-awaited day arrived — and was I glad? Eddie had been on pins himself and so were the lads taking the trip with us, and why not? It was a good time and a good thing to go home to our loved ones, and we all knew it.

Our morning had dawned, as all mornings do and we managed to eat a little food, have a last minute chat with a few of the third party, then we strolled onto the upper deck to wait the last half hour. Eventually, everybody was ready. The launch and tugs came alongside to carry us across to the landing where we were to pick the steamer up. One by one we were called from the list and descended into the waiting transport, and then to wait until the steamer came. That came soon after we arrived, conveying with it the returning leave party. I saw Dave for a second as he came from the ship and out into the launch to be carried back to the *Furious*. As the last man left, we began to climb aboard. There were quite a number of people and it was a lovely morning; the sea was much calmer than the first time I crossed it but that would not worry me very much now after the storms we had been through while in the Arctic. Our ship was just like a cork upon the ocean and I can say that sometimes it made me quite ill. One minute you would be on top of a huge wave, then the next, deep down between two sea mountains. It was on a day much as this that a very funny thing happened. Our Commanding Officer of the forecastle was with me and another lad tightening ropes and other loose articles about the upper deck when in a flash a great dark shadow came over us. We looked up to see a massive tower of green water rushing towards us. Someone screamed to us, 'Hold on to something, there's a wave coming on board!' The warning came a little too late as we had already seen the damage. The wave hit us with such a furious sounding roar, completely swamping the decks and with it, we were thrown along the deck rolling over and over. I got jammed in a corner and hung onto something firm like grim death, but where I was no one could see me. So when the water cleared from the decks, I appeared to be missing and before I could gather my wits about me, I heard someone shout, 'Rogers is gone sir. The wave must have got him. Any use calling away the boats?' I heard the dim, faint voice of the officer saying, 'Not in this sea?'

With this, I gave a cry out. 'Here I am! Tangled among these ropes and wires. It's alright I am not hurt, just wet.'

I saw the officer's face light up and with a sigh of relief he only said, 'Thank God for a miracle.'

I could still see his face when Eddie hit me on the side of the head saying, 'Cheer up, Fred, you will be back to the ship in fourteen days.' We both laughed and saw the steamer move slowly away out towards the mainland and at that moment I got a nasty pain across my temple. I touched the spot and found I had a deep gash just above my left ear. Eddie noticed the sudden change of my expression. He discovered the wound and immediately called over the Petty Officer at hand. He was one of the older ratings and had been with the ship since it was first launched, I thought to myself as he examined the bleeding gash. The PO told Lofty to get me down to the shower and see that I got cleaned up and take me along to the sick bay for whatever treatment was needed.

Away we went below decks to get the dirty gear off and shower. I felt a bit lightheaded as I stripped off my clothes and went to get into the shower, but Lofty suddenly grabbed my arm and told me I sure had a good body for a young kid. I pulled away and got into the shower, but he dragged me to the bulkhead without me turning on the water. I yelled at him to stop fooling around as he pressed himself against me pretty savagely and again, I yelled at him to stop getting our flag poles at half mast and leave my Union Jack anchored down and forget this bloody nonsense. With a savage thrust he pushed me against the ship's side and did I see stars! I must have given my head a nasty bump and passed out. When I came to, there were a few lads around me and a towel had been thrown over me. I heard one lad say that I must have knocked myself out. I asked one of the lads where was Lofty? No one seemed to know. They found me sprawled out on the deck. I heard Eddie's voice telling someone about the accident with the huge wave and the Petty Officer giving Lofty instructions to get me below and for me to get cleaned up before being taken to sick bay. Another lad said it might be time to get me to the sick bay and that is what they did. All this time I began to wonder whether I'd dreamt the attack on me and if it was real or not. My head was still giving me a fantastic light show and I felt rotten and dirty. I was patched up and given the towel to wrap around my middle and marched off to the mess deck. I never did mention Lofty's antics to anyone and I'm sure he didn't get what he was after, so I let the incident creep into the back of my mind and locked the door.

The trip was a calm one and the sea matched the blue sky; I was hoping it would be nice when we got home. From the deck rail, we spoke of the last few months and what lay ahead of us in the years to come. The hours passed away like the wind over the meadow and we were preparing to land in next to no time. We were given another meal in the Thurso Town Hall, which went down very nicely indeed and then had about an hour and a half to wait for our train, so we wandered about at our leisure among the quaint houses and lovely shops. We sat on a small set of stones outside some cottages and the owners spoke to us and offered food and drink. They were really swell people. The time slipped by again and as we heard the train coming up towards the station, we got into line with the rest of the lads and watched the incoming passengers alight. When the word was given, we all took our turn getting into our seats and settled down for our long trip from one end of the country to almost the other.

I was very glad the weather was nice for our trip. It makes travelling all that much better, and you can always look away across the countryside and wonder what everybody was doing. I always like reading on trains, makes the trip seem shorter if the weather is bad, but having Eddie with me on the trip this time, all we did was talk. Town after town came and went and as the houses flew by, we began to get hungry. The train came to a stop in one of the Scottish cities for meal bags and hot tea for us, that gave us heart again to get along with our journey. Day turned into night and back again to day, and after half of the next morning had gone by, we began to get ready for the change of trains. The time we lost in changing trains was not a great deal and we were soon rushing towards our hometown. The trip had begun to get boring by late afternoon and when at last we did arrive at our destination, we were fed up, but to see the train leave the platform was a comfort and we began our walk to town. The last bus had surely gone, so with our cases and gas masks we left the station and walked.

Eddie went his way and I went mine, to get to the house only to wake everyone up. Everyone welcomed me with all the usual fuss, it was great and at last I managed to get to bed which I needed more at that moment than anything else in the whole world.

The weather was really good for us at last, every time I managed to get near home it turned out wet, but the morning after we arrived it was swell. My first thought was the swimming pool. It had been a very long time since I was warm enough to swim but this day seemed perfect, so away I went. It was only a few minutes from my home to the pool so I was well-off. I really did enjoy myself that summer morning. There were only a few at the pool this time of day, but I knew most of them and we got down to more talking than swimming but it was nice sitting on the bank in the sun. Lunch time came about before we were aware of it. I made up my mind to spend quite a lot of time down at the pool. The evenings I devoted to Edna and dancing — she was, of course, working and was not free until the evenings. We went dancing most nights, but one or two we had for our films. Dancing was our greatest joy, and so were the evenings strolling home — but of course that is an entirely different story. Anyway, my leave was slipping away right from under my very eyes and there seemed so much I still wanted to do, but we just had a good time. Edna and I met Eddie on our last day's leave and we all came home to tea and that ended another smashing leave. Not very exciting I admit, but to me it was wonderful just to be home safe in body and mind. Edna and my sister, Mill, came to the railroad station to see Eddie and I off. Watching them from the carriage window, I wondered when I could see them again, but it was not too far in distance, not soon enough for Christmas but just nice for the New Year's tidings.

As usual, the train journey back to the ship was not the excitement of my leave at home which I had just the fondest memories. The small market town that I had grown up in was dear to my heart. Many a lonely night on watch I would walk the narrow streets of Pontypool drinking in the sweet dreams of times spent glancing at the great pubs with their equally great names. I passed The New Moon, which always made me smile; it was on a night of another new moon I thought of telling Edna how much she meant to me. Other pubs I passed with fond memories, but funnily enough I never did get to set foot in any of them. The park was my very favourite place because years and years ago I took part in the county's school carnival, my sister dressed me up as Sir Walter Raleigh and I was told I looked just dandy. I had always taken an interest in history and knew about the time Sir Walter had laid down his cloak for Queen Elizabeth I to tread on. This act I carried out in the park to the cheering of the happy people, and low and behold I got first prize.

The train gave a sudden shudder tossing me out of my favourite dream — must have been a sheep on the line, I thought. It did not take me long to fall to dreaming again. Edna came to mind, sweet Edna, then my brother Ken came into focus and the day the three of us spent at the pool. Ken was very proud of his young brother for going off to the wars and I felt a little sorry for him because the job he had, protected him from going into the forces. He had been a coal miner, as was my dad most of his working life. He seemed content with the way the war had served him and he always told me that his job was just as important as mine was. The days we three spent at the swimming pool were great. He got on very well with Edna, and Edna likewise. Ken was a bit of a loveable larrikin, he would tease Edna about not liking to wear a bathing suit. I understood her feelings because she didn't have the voluptuous figure of Ester Williams or the style of Lana Turner, but to me she was the next best thing to an angel. Ken would suddenly, at a moment's notice, take off to the diving board and do some of the funniest tricks before making a mountain of splashes, intending of course to shower our dry bathers with cold water.

The train stopped suddenly and whistles were blowing in every direction. It was only warnings about air raids and the paraphernalia of wartime rules. My daydreams of home leave left me somehow a little sad. Eddie sensed my sadness and gave me a dig in the ribs. He promised me that things would look nice and rosy when I eventually got back home and cuddled up to Edna — that I did look forward to. Sighing deeply, I took his advice and joined him in laughter but I dared not think of the long trip back to the island., I just let the train carry us on and on into the night and day. It's a good job I like reading in trains or else I may have gone off my head with all those miles of travelling to go. It had been warm that day and it was not by any means comfortable waiting for your journey's end. But as always, it does come. I found myself back in Scapa among the large and small vessels, we passed the third and last leave party on the landing waiting for the steamer to carry them off. The same old saucy remarks were made and then we were off towards the old *Furious* and somehow not sorry to be back aboard. Everything was how we had left it and with Dave still carrying on with his switchboard, I went down to see him as soon as I got aboard. He was on watch at the time; he was just down below my flat and had a steel ladder down to it from one end. As I got down there, I wondered who had been doing my work while I was away because there had been no one in my beloved flat rubbing and scrubbing away and singing to my heart's content. I would soon have the place looking as if I had never left, and by the end of the week I was right. The weather had held rather nicely, so Eddie and I planned a walk for Sunday morning after the service, roaming around the lanes and rocks of Flotta; this was the nearest island in the group to our ship and it was the only one we were allowed to visit, except on special occasions. It boasted of wet and dry canteens, a cinema and a pebble beach, and it was fun on a warm day. We had our fun by playing the age-old 'Ducks and Drakes' and the walks were alright, but you would not find much grass or any trees. It really is a very funny bit of land, just off the tip of Scotland, but like a world of its own; you would not call its sunrise or sunset lovely, but yet when you happened to be there at the right moment, it held you just as they did in the tropics — which I was to find out very soon. Anyway, the weeks flew by and before we knew it, summer was beginning to pick up her skirts and slide softly off. And as she slipped away, she left in the air that nip which warned us that Jack Frost would soon be on the loose again bringing with him the cold winds and the snow. I was hoping to be away from Scapa before the cold winter set in. The last one was enough for me and then the memories of Norway came back with its greatness and untold beauty. We were not doing these trips anyway now; things had got a little quiet of late, that was at least until one night I thought it was going to be quiet. I had just slung my hammock, got in, intending to have a sleep, when all of a sudden I was shaken and surprised to hear the sounding of 'Action Stations'. I thought I was dreaming and began to settle down again, but that was short-lived. The Captains of the Guns were busy, rushing around getting us to our posts without more to do. It was cold too, and no one was in any good mood being rushed about the place in the middle of the night, not knowing what it was all about. But we soon did: a neat and daring trick had been pulled off by the Germans. They had sent a sub, or subs, into the harbour of Scapa through the nets and traps and were at that moment among our ships watching and waiting to strike. Our radar had picked them up passing through the defence and they were, at the moment, picking out whatever ship they pleased to attack and blow it sky high. Most of the ships were dropping depth chargers and smoke screens. Boats were out watching and waiting for goodness knows what. By morning, we had not located these subs, but neither had they attacked any of our ships. They surely must have slipped out again by now as easily as they had come in! But then it dawned on us, perhaps they were mine laying in Scapa Flow! What an affair, with the Flow alive with mines every ship would be sunk under our very noses. We were all given sailing orders very soon after this, and so we were off again to Scotland while the Flow was swept for mines. I was very pleased to be going back to Scotland again. I had had a very nice time at the place I was at when last in Scotland and was looking forward to my return. Eddie and I set about getting ready for our trip ashore. Eddie and I could always find fun wherever we went, and this time we would try our best. We arrived in very wet weather and while we were at this port it did not seem to get much better. A few nice films, shows and dances were had by us both; the folks were jolly and everything went well. We spent quite a lot of time ashore for after being in Scapa Flow, a change was very good indeed. Every time we were due for our turns ashore, we would take it and each evening we returned to our club for a good laugh and talk. Next morning, we had to be up early to catch the boat to take us back to the ship in time to begin the day's work and carrying on until our next run ashore. But our stay was not a very long one, and when we were given the all clear to enter Scapa again, we all took the last look at good old Scotland and sailed back to our treeless sanctuary.

Cold winds were sweeping Scapa as we arrived back from our short stay in Scotland, reminding us perhaps to get ready for more snow within a few months. I was thinking of my next winter in England with all the rain and cold winds around — everywhere you went the weather was cold. The only thing to do about this was to get out of the country and find some place hot. I smiled at this, but if I could have known my life story for the next six months, I may have thought differently. But then at that moment, all those dreams and warm climates were very far off, so I just laughed it off and began to put the much troubled and lazy mind to work. A few weeks more of quiet and peaceful duties and October came to an end, and with it very sad news. The *Furious*, being an old warship, was to be taken away from the sea and her crew and to end her days under the mighty hand of the men to whom comes the job of breaking up. This news was very distressing and meant quite a lot of partying among the fellows, also it was the parting of Dave and I and also Eddie. I only saw them both a few times in England after that and it took a long time for me to get used to things without them. We all had such smashing times aboard and ashore, all the crew were in well with each other, and me and my flat would have to part as well. The day came for stripping down the ship, and what a job we all made of it. Everything removable was taken away, memory after memory came and went. The fun, laughter and almost tears must have gone through everyone's minds, but this had to be, and the ship really was getting old, it was about time she gave in. I shall never forget the good times I had and as we went through the days stripping her down, I almost wished I could get my draft right away and remember her as I had always known her: very busy, always waiting for the next trip out to the cold waters of the Arctic. A few lads had been given their drafts but not many, we were all too busy stripping the ship. Eddie and I were not in our flats anymore, they were up to our necks in dirt and waste, all the gear was being carried out and I never went near the Flow very often. We still had our old talks up on deck in the evening, making the most of them now. We never knew what would become of us. As soon as we left the ship, we could have been posted to different points of the globe. We each had one another's home address and that was the only way we would be able to trace each other. And so, when the time of parting arrived, everybody took it on the chin and said goodbye to the *Furious* for the last time.

EMBARKATION LEAVE

Now that the *Furious* was out of sight, but not out of mind, we were at a loss to what we were going to do. I had lost touch with Dave and Eddie a few days after arriving in barracks, so I was completely lost. I did not greet Plymouth at the best of times, but there it was, I was there so I had to take it with a smile.

Luck was still with me. I had only been in barracks about a week when quite a number of us were given draft chits to a camp just outside Plymouth in a small village that sounded much better than staying in Plymouth itself. It was twenty-five miles outside the city. The name of the village was Yealmpton and we soon got settled in there, but the weather was cold and wet. The end of November was almost here, and the sign of snow was in the air; frost had already taken the place of fog and the clear cold air at night made me think of Christmas. A white Christmas was never in the question as I had only seen one white Christmas and that was when I was very young, but anyway the lads in my hut were jolly chaps. One was from Canada, he was always joking and did not feel the cold as much as we did. As regards to work, there was never very much of it except for the outside working parties which were working out of camp in the nearby villages. They had Saturdays and Sundays off with no duty watch, so it was considered a good number. We did alright in the camp and we never went far after we had finished work at four. The wet, cold nights had most of the lads staying at camp. There was a cinema at the other end and sometimes we would go there, if the films were any good. In the village they sometimes had a good dance on, but as I said, I was mostly in the hut writing and reading. This kind of life had been going on until about the middle of December when one day I was called to the office. As I got there, I was told I had been put on the Foreign Services Pool, waiting for a ship to go abroad. This of course was very good news. Everyone waits for the time when they can go abroad. Two other lads from our huts were put in the pool as well and the next bit of good news I received that day was to tell me I had been put on the outside working party. Right away I thought of Saturdays and Sundays off, no more duty watch at night. I was doing quite alright, the only trouble was I could not have any long leave while I was in the 'Pool', this meant of course, no Christmas leave. It did not sound very grand, but still it was not the end of the world and a Naval Christmas is not too bad, so I soon got used to the idea.

My new job was in a small village just beyond the one we were in and it consisted of laying a siding for a small railroad, we all had a grand time over it. Hot meals were supplied at midday. The weather was cold at first, but we soon warmed up, clearing away sand and dirt. I really enjoyed those few weeks of hard work. It made us hungry so we ate more and were healthier for it. We were out in the open air all day until 5 pm when we would be taken back to camp in the truck, and the rest of the evening was our own until 8 am the next morning. It did me the world of good, but my mind was forever on the subject of going abroad, and going where?

I was soon to find out, because one morning a few days before Christmas, I went up to the office to put my card in after we had finished work (this was to tell who had left the camp through the day. You had to collect the card in the evenings before you went ashore, then as you went ashore, you again handed them in until you arrived back. This kept a check on everybody).

I was called over by the Chief and he said, 'You have finished on this job Rogers, come back up here at ten-thirty and you shall get your sailing orders.'

I said with great excitement, 'Where am I going, Chief?'

All he said was in a matter-of-fact tone, 'I think to the "Golden Hind".'

At that moment, the name meant no more to me than the man in the moon. So, I just went back to the hut and waited for the most important news in my life as of date. No one was up when I entered the hut because the working parties are up early, before the rest of the camp. The hut was in darkness, so I went slowly back to my bed and lay there wondering who else would be going. I was one of the first to know. Because of my working early, would the other lads in our hut go too? It would be grand for us all to go together, we had been having good times since being together in that hut. We went to a few dances in the village hall and were soon the best of pals with a few of the girls, this made things perfect for dancing over the Christmas time, and with the holidays close at hand, we had been planning what to do. A few parties were to be put on, and dances with all the food free for Christmas Day for the forces so it did not sound too bad. Going into Plymouth would not be too good. There were far too many lads there already so our best plan was to stay in the country; I was still thinking about all this when 'Reveille' was sounded off. This meant rise and shine. The weather had managed to keep fine all that night and consequently, there was a very thick frost, the wet road had been turned to ice and every tree was also covered in ice. They were still wet from the rain the afternoon before, the fields were likewise and for the first look out, you had the impression that the place was covered in a mantle of snow and the sky looked all set for it too. Were we going to have snow for Christmas after all, then? Before we got an answer to that, I had a pillow thrown in my face and someone shouting, 'What's wrong with you, lazy? Forgot to go to work this morning, wait until the old chief catches up with you!' Ray had been the culprit with the pillow, so I flung it back, hitting someone else and they began to tell my tale of the Golden Hind. Ray was one of my pals whom I had met in the hut and we were the two who had done all the arranging with the girls. He was a North Welshman and a very good pal.

The usual, 'Wishing I was coming with you' saying went on, but I don't think they thought for a minute that within a very few hours a few of their sayings would come true. They all strolled out into the cold morning to begin their day's work of tidying up the camp, while I and a few of the hut cleaners built a fire in the stove and got things clean about the place. It was a change to be in the warm hut of a morning instead of out in the cold and wind and I was now waiting for my Passage and the weekend would bring Christmas.

The time was just at 'stand easy' and almost time for me to

be getting up to the office when in popped a messenger with a chit for Ray and another of our pals to be at the office by 10.30 am for our sailing orders abroad. At the same moment, the lads came in for 'stand easy' so Ray walked right into this draft notice also and I laughed and said, 'You, too, can have a tropical kit like mine.' So away we trotted to the Master-At-Arms office to await our fate. There were quite a number of lads already up there and within a few minutes of our arrival, the Chief began to call our names out one by one. We were told of our departure from the Port at Liverpool on the liner *Dominion Monarch* early in the New Year and within a few days we would be off on leave for two weeks. Our destination was Golden Hind in the city of Sydney, Australia. What luck! Ray and I, with the others, were off to the land of sunshine, plenty to eat and hot smashing weather, and by leaving in January we would just catch the middle of summer. So now that the good news was told, all we had to wait for was January. I would not be home for Christmas, but would be there for New Year. I wrote home and said I was coming a few days after Christmas but could not write about our sailing to Australia. No one knew the sailing date, so it could not be told. We were very busy getting attended to by the doctors and other medical folk that it was Christmas before we looked around, and so all work stopped for a few days and we all went to church on Christmas morning. Lunch was a smashing feast. The rest of the day we were ashore and as I have already said, Ray and I had our dates; we all had a jolly good time walking through the country and making our fun on the way. The village held a dance in the evening, the pub did a good trade as usual and on the whole it was one of the best Christmas tides I have ever spent. It always took quite a time to arrive, but it went so quickly from right under your nose. Boxing Day came and went and the whole concern passed very quickly. The girls did not like the idea of us leaving for Australia, but I thought it was the best thing that could happen; I was really fed up with the snow and cold weather. I was glad I did not have to spend the whole of the winter in England and as each day passed by, they got slower. The day we left camp for our last leave was not too bad though, we knew that every leave goes far too quickly. We were not in any bad mood, as no one expected these two weeks at home. I had let the folks know what time I would be arriving so I was sure of a nice cup of tea when I got back.

The trip never did seem so long to me, and when I arrived at the station, I was a little tired. I was lucky I did not have to walk from the rail station, as usually I would have had to at that time of night. There was a van doing a little late work and it happened to be passing just as I was thinking of the long walk in front of me. The man stopped and asked if I wanted a lift, which I very soon told him that I did, and could he take me as far as the town post office? I was very grateful for that lift, I did not have a great way to go after that, just over half a mile. My kit was not too comfortable but I managed to drag myself home to find the folks had waited up for me. I soon got down to the meal that had been prepared for me and gee it was good. I had scattered my things all over the house. Gas mask in one corner, coat and cap in another, a case here and a kit bag there. Every time I arrived home the place was upside down. We spoke for a little while, about how long I was home for, why I had come home so soon, where was I going after getting back? No one liked the idea of my trip to

Australia but I told them it was a wonderful thing and I was as pleased as punch about it. They did not mind so much afterwards, and in a short while after I had eaten my meal I was off to bed. Home again after fifteen months in the Navy, time really did slip by, I could remember the day I first went from the house to join the force, cold and damp. It was again cold that evening, the last days of December; the air was as clear as a bell and as I thought about these things, I must have dropped off to sleep for I remembered nothing else until late the next morning. Everyone was down before me. New Year's Eve, and everything was alive and bright. I wanted to visit some very good friends of mine so off I strolled after a little meal to see Olive and George — very nice people, full of life and with always the welcome sign on the door mat. Marie was their daughter, a little younger than myself, very nice and we both had always been the best of friends. There was a lot of talk going around at one time or another regarding the two of us, but with little foundation.

Anyway, I always kept my first visit for them and we all had jolly good times together. We have always done so in the past and I hope always in the future. Leave at home always seems important to me, all your old friends you see and talk to, quite a good time is had and with your best pal you can talk over all that you have missed since being home last. But this leave was to be without my pal, for the same morning I came home he joined the army and was gone hours before I arrived home, and that meant I was not to see him for quite a long time. I did not know it then, but it was to be over two years before we both met on leave. I was to do a lot of travelling before that date. Where, how and when I did not know, but I got to find out very soon after my leave was up. The New Year came with the usual joy and fun-making, parties and wine were to be found for the short while. I was enjoying myself with Olive and George at their home in the evening, full of life there, and by the time the party was breaking up it was no longer New Year's Eve, but New Year's Day. That night there was more fun and everyone I met would say, 'Having a good time?' Or, 'When are you going back?' Questions such as these drove me nuts, almost. The folks who said them should be given six months, some of the lads would say. I always smiled to myself when I thought of the lads trying to give some poor old sole six months for asking, 'When are you going back?'

The dances were good too on this leave and everything was at its best. The only things missing were Ray and the fun we both always had. I had got his address from his mother and we were soon at it with the usual talk of, 'How do you like the Navy? When are you coming home? Where are you going to be stationed?' All the old topics in the world we found to talk about.

My time to leave was getting closer and that meant I would have to make up a lot of time in the last few days. I went to my last dance with Edna the night before I left, and we promised to meet the next day, but I thought it would be better to leave without seeing her again. So, I left without seeing her and after leaving her the night before, I did not know when we would meet again. I did not dream we would meet at the place where we did though, quite a distance from the place where I last saw her. But that was looking too far ahead. We shall cross those bridges when we come to them.

Parting from the folks, that last leave was of course a little different as I did not really know when I would see them again.

I kept telling them I was looking forward to going and that I should be alright and I was old enough to look after myself. I had spent my nineteenth birthday off the coast of Norway and I was determined to be able to take care of myself and look after my own affairs. I could not blame my family for being worried, I suppose it was only natural for them, so with a smile and a word of good cheer, I was away again on the road to adventure and I knew it was going to be hard, long and very dangerous, the world was at my shoulder.

I SAIL WITH THE DOMINION MONARCH

The rushing around that awaited me when I got back to camp was very tiresome, we were all to be ready to leave for Liverpool in two days, which would make the date January 14th, and we were embarking aboard the liner *Dominion Monarch* leaving on the 19th bound for the city of Sydney, New South Wales, Australia. We had just opened a new RN camp called Golden Hind, our group were to be known as 'J3', a kind of Naval code number, so the first thing I had to do was rush down to the hut and get back to the clothing store as soon as possible. I was getting all my tropical kit that day and different cards and papers, I got my hammock and kit painted with a huge red line so that officials knew at a glance I was heading to Australia — everybody who was leaving on the same ship as I was were in the same mad rush, and by the time night fell, I was completely exhausted, what with the train journey and the new gear I had to get together. I was very much fed up. The next day promised to be just as busy with doctors and dentists. Vaccinations were plentiful and with that rushing through my mind, I fell asleep, far away from the night before and feeling a little bit bored with things but the reminder of our voyage to the land of the sun I felt as happy as a king. However happy that should be. Anyway the next morning found us waiting to see the doctor and the dentist as well as a dozen or more other people, questions, answers, writing, labelling, packing, last minute washing. Letters to write but still no information about what we were doing and above all no sailing date, we would be allowed to write home a week out at sea and give our new address in Australia. Until then, silence! We could say what we were feeling like and talk about the weather but not very much to help those at home who were wondering when we would be sailing away.

That last day finally came to an end, and with the coming of the morrow we were to be up at the gates ready with all our gear to push off to the station in the barracks at Plymouth. There was a private station inside Devonport Barracks for big drafts like ours, this made things a lot easier for everyone: no walking about, no kit to carry and no town to cross, just get into the train and off. I had earned my last sleep in camp and I was ready for it. My kit had been stacked with the rest, ready for carting away to barracks in the morning. I only had to take my gear that I needed on the voyage when I went up to fall in the next day, so a little pleased at the thought of no rushing around the camp. I again took to slumber and let the dawn bring what it may.

We arose to find that the frost had given way to very fine rain, a lovely pickle to be in when you are moving about, it should not rain hard I was hoping because our kit would get wet but still it did not look very much like rain and with a last hurried look at the clouds I began to get ready for the short trip to the barracks.

I was one of the first to get all my gear together and be waiting at the Office of the Mate at Arms. Some of us had been ready for a long time. Ray as usual was late, no matter how important an affair was he would never be on time. He would probably be late for his own wedding! I would not be a bit surprised. Anyway, at last everyone was there, our names were called and recalled. The trucks were waiting so one by one we took our turn getting aboard the trucks, kits all on and with a last look around the grey, cold camp, we rushed down the lanes and out to the open highway.

Barracks was exactly as I had left it a little while ago, the tall building looking grim and unfriendly with the guards all around — it always made me shudder. Talk about prison! It reminded me of just that, but I knew from my other visits that once inside, the lads were a jolly bunch, full of fun and you always had something to do. Of course we were not there to stay, so everyone of us were taken to the gym and told to get comfortable until we were ready for the train. That was not too long to wait for, we each were given numbers and instructions and in turn went to the barrack station and boarded the train. Our long journey to Liverpool was about to begin. Quite a number of the chaps were hanging around shouting goodbyes to pals and some wishing they were coming along, and as our train slid out of the station onto the main lines, I said to myself, 'I wonder when I shall be seeing Devonport again?'

The train was rushing along at a great speed to make the journey as quick as possible. The only thing I did not like about it was that we had to pass through my hometown. I was hoping it would not stop. Let's get going, no reminders of home at a time like this. Somehow, I had lost Ray while getting on the train, so I had no one I knew very well to speak to for a while, but he soon found me and we managed to get together. There were a few lads that always went about with Ray and myself so everything was alright. I had spotted another lad whom I knew aboard the train too, not very well but he had been on the *Furious* and I made up my mind to speak to him when we met again, which of course was to be very soon. He was on the same train, going to the same camp in Australia so we were bound to see each other. The train still rushed us through towns, cities, villages and county sides. It all looked so peaceful from my carriage window, who would think that war and devastation was ruling with an iron hand? These cottages, these streets, all may have been under the enemy's heel. But for only one thing and that was because it was British, no one would take this Island from us until every man jack of us had perished.

My mind had been wandering around for a while, I thought, because when I came back to myself, we were pulling into one of the big city stations for snacks and tea. Here was where I met Frank from the *Furious*. We smiled and I said, 'You remember me of course.' He had seen me on board so we were soon talking about old times. We really did talk a lot in those five minutes on the station, we were to look out for each other at Liverpool. I had my mouth full of food as we said our cheerios. Ray had saved some tea for me which I was glad of as I had completely forgotten to get some when I was talking to Frank. His home was in Bristol, not such a great distance from my home. Ray said he saw I was too busy talking and that I had no tea so we got down to drinking it and by the time it had gone, and the food had disappeared, we were again in the English countryside, where the flat fields and the tall tress met the grey sky of a January afternoon. Just to think that in about a week we would be in lovely sunshine right across the Atlantic and nearing the Panama Canal. It did not seem right, when you look at this winter of ours, it looked as if it would be snowing at any moment. With the high winds and the bare branches on all the trees, it was hard to believe that very soon it would be giving way to sunlight, blue skies and tropical lands, but before the calm always comes a storm!

We were now approaching the South Wales lines and within an hour we would be passing through my hometown. The Severn Tunnel came and went and now we were passing through the small Welsh towns and as we passed, the lads would try to pronounce the names and what a mess they would make of them. We were now passing factories and steel works where a good many of my pals were working at that very moment, also the glass factory where I used to work that was right outside the hometown station and before I knew what was happening, the train had pulled up and stopped right in the station. What rotten luck! If I had of known that was going to happen, my folks could have come down and seen me again for a few minutes. It was to be exactly fifteen minutes.

Ray would have to come out with the words, 'Why don't you jump, Fred?'

I said, 'Thanks very much, pal, but I don't think the Admiralty would like that somehow,' and with those words we pulled out of the station and I watched the old hometown fade in the distance. The hum of the engine seemed to be saying, 'You will see it all again one day.' Wales soon slipped past my window and I was too tired to be taking in everything I saw, so I tried to get a little sleep — and little was right. Trying to get some sleep on a troop train is like trying to buy ham and eggs where there are no shops, so after trying for a while I gave up and got out my book, reading I don't know what. Ray seemed to be very busy with something he was writing so I could not talk with him. I felt really bored and to think within a few days I would be out of all this cold and damp, smiling at the memories of winter. Thinking of these things did not help whatsoever and with a sigh I got back down to staring out of the carriage window. The countryside was changing now, the buildings and towns were getting more crowded and smoky, the places looked as if they all wanted a good deal of sunshine. Ahead I saw through the mist a silver line and realised it must be the sea somewhere about Liverpool.

I felt a little brighter and within half an hour of getting ready, we arrived into town and the sea port of Liverpool. Of course, it was dark by this time and there was not much to be seen, only tall towers and buildings, ships in the distance and the smell of salt water came to me as soon as I stepped off the train. I may have imagined that of course for we had a bus journey to get over yet before arriving at the docks where our ship was waiting for us. It was cold too on that station after the warm atmosphere of the train, but I was glad to get out and walk. All day in a train is quite enough for me, not forgetting the train journeys to Scapa Flow the year before. Anyway, the buses were at the station entrance and we set about getting to the docks. All our kit was being taken care of by vans and trucks. I got a glimpse of Frank in the crowd but since I last spoke to him on the train just after we pulled out of Hereford, I hadn't had a chance to speak to him again. I would most probably see him on board anyway, it would take a few weeks to get across. The buses were very busy with the lot of us that night, we were not the only ones going aboard the *Dominion Monarch*. It took more than that night to get the last man aboard but after waiting our turn for a bus, we got under way through dark streets and lonely by-ways. Huge, sinister warehouses towered on both sides of the streets, then a few shops and houses, we had missed the centre of Liverpool and by doing so it would save time no doubt. I was wondering about all this when the bus stopped outside what appeared to me to be a dirty-looking shed. Such a look at this time of night made me think of my nice warm bed at home. To make things look worse, there was a fine drizzle and this time of night made it a lot more different to get on with.

The time was 11.30 pm and we had to get checked off, given deck numbers to tell us what part of the ship we were to go to. The draft number, as I said before, was 'J3'. The shipload of us were known as this number, there seemed to be quite a lot more people around inside the sheds and as we passed through the gates, a bunch of girls waiting around to thrill everyone were giving all the lads a kiss each and it went down very well. Some did not bother about the girls but of course Ray and I got to thinking that if they wanted to kiss us, we were not going to be spoilsports. Ray, by this time, had had more than his share so I pushed him aside and had more than my share. We got around to seeing the different officers in charge, getting orders for the voyage, what to do and what not to do. We were on the Promenade Deck and incidentally we had the bathing pool on our deck. I did not know this until the next morning. At last we were passing the last officer and then out into the open wharf and right before us was the towering giant with its great two funnels. At last we were climbing the gang-way to the liner *Dominion Monarch*. We walked through the foyer and other parts of this lovely vessel until we came to the dining hall and we ate a very nice hot meal at 12.30 am. When at last we got ourselves settled down for sleep, it must have been going on 2 am. At last, everything was quiet. For the first time in my life I was sleeping in a giant liner waiting for the nineteenth so we could go sailing from one end of the world to the other. Australia here we come!

FIRST VOYAGE TO AUSTRALIA

The two days we were in Liverpool waiting to leave was almost thrilling and of course it was something new to us. Living on a liner really was smashing, walking along the decks and rooms of this great ship was like something from another world. I thought of all the folks that had walked these very decks in peacetime, sailing around the world, fun and joy everywhere. But now, it was not quite like that; the decks were cold and wet from the January rain and snow. No well-dressed pair strolling along, bellboys with their usual small trays, all gone and in their stead uniforms on their way far across the sea to win a war that must — and will — be won.

Dreaming of the days that used to be found me wandering to the stern of the ship where I came across a swimming pool. It looked very nice but that too was now disused and empty. It looked really good though and before the trip was over, we were to have lots of fun around and about that pool. Ray and Frank were near me in our billets on board, so we had each other to talk to, and to make our own fun. We would go up on deck and gaze out over the Liverpool waters and talk ourselves to death, almost! It was cold and wet these last few days, but we stuck it out and got our fill of England, goodness knows when we would see it again. The city looked sad from where we were and before we were to see the last of it, the wet streets and buildings were to be turned into a white postcard. My last look of an English storm of snow for a few years.

The nineteenth dawned with grey and red skies, but it was fine, with an icy wind. I can still feel the suspense and excitement of our sailing day. Although it was winter and the sky was grey, it felt like a lush spring morning. Everybody was on deck hours before we were ready to sail but eventually the dull, hollow sound of the ship's foghorn sang over the waters and within a second or two we began to move. At the same moment the snow fell — and it really did fall. Blowing onto the decks and covering everybody that stood in its path. We watched the buildings from across the water turn white and the snow kept coming down. It was still falling when the last patch of land disappeared from sight among the clouds and mist. Our folks would now have to stay in our memory, and the dreams of the future, where now we may be going were about to come true. This trip through the oceans of the world was going to be a landmark in all our lives.

The weather did not break up very well, the snow had stopped but we were left with a very heavy swell for days. The ship turned and tossed with bitter cold winds so we did not do very much for the first week but stay below decks. I had seen the cold Atlantic in a temper scores of times before and this crossing I was leaving out. We enjoyed ourselves though; films, games, talks and lots of books to read and soon we would be reaching Colón and the Panama Canal then it would be much warmer, and indeed as each day passed the cold winds began to die down. The swell left off its fury and the clouds broke to find us in a calm sea, blue sky and a smashing sun, mid January and we were enjoying at last, much better than any mid summer weather you may find in England!

That called for sunbathing and out everybody came. It was grand to walk along the decks amid the dazzling sun, sky and sea. The flying fish were in great numbers and it was something new and funny to watch. First you saw a flash of silver, then closer you saw wings and a fish, then it was gone to be followed by another and yet another. I watched them for hours on end, and now and again a branch of palm tree would float past then long seaweed, which of course would indicate that not so very far away was land. It was just over a week since we left Liverpool and it seemed to have been a lifetime, the change in the weather had quite a lot to do with that. Ray and I would sit on the ledge of the swimming pool and talk of home but would end by talking of Australia. He had seen most of my snaps of the girls and the folks I knew, and I had seen all of his, and by these we had grown to know each other even more than before. We were at the same old spot one morning when the coastline of Central America came in sight and then Colón the gateway to the Panama, we arrived in the middle of the rain season and it was raining when the ship docked. We were to stay twenty-four hours, for fresh provisions the American forces were there, very busy with their crafts and motorboats, talking and fun went on among our lads and the 'Yanks'. The natives were busy throwing fruit up to us from the wharfs such as bananas and oranges, fruit we had almost forgotten about and in exchange we threw coins to them. Some were far below while others were on the rooftops of the wharf blowing and crying out such strange noises making us laugh and asking for more. Then, to our joy, a notice was posted up on the grand stairway to the dining room letting everyone know we could go ashore that afternoon. The dress was to be tropical shirt and shorts. It was to be grand, setting foot for the first time on real foreign soil, and American soil at that. So, we at once got down to preparing for our afternoon ashore. I did not see Frank, so Ray and I could not ask him to come along.

The weather was very warm and the smell of the rain on the hot ground was very refreshing indeed. We were all on the upper deck waiting for the word 'go' right on time and as these few words were sounded off, everybody was away down the gangway and indeed it was good to set foot on land again. It was almost two weeks since we left Liverpool amid the winter storms and now we were out in Colón amid the hot sunny rain showers. It was kind of monsoon weather this part of the world was having, so we were expecting to get wet any minute, but we were fairly lucky because we were only caught in one nice shower and that was while we were returning to the ship anyway! We went walking through the wharf and side buildings for the use of baggage from the ships and food stuffs from all parts of the world. Ray and I took in what we were able to see and being in the lovely hot sun was something in itself. The palm trees and coconuts being thrown by the monkeys were really a laugh, everybody seemed to be enjoying the walk out in the fresh air and when the evening drew near there was to be an American show. The place was so different from what we had been used to so it interested us so much that time seemed to fly by and time for the show was drawing near so when Ray and I arrived at the appointed place, quite a number of lads had already been waiting.

This show went off smashing and the lads loved it, no one can put a show over like the Yanks and they gave a jitterbug contest which was right down some of our lads' streets and they gave the showgirls a dance for their money. Free drinks were provided for us all at the end of the show, the American Way, and there is something about that which has to be different.

Walking back to our now brightly-lit ship was worth a good memory, the sky needed no more glamour to make everything more beautiful. It was just as if it was a painting, but we did not know how quickly an evening could turn very wet and in a twinkle of an eye, we were walking in torrents of rain and everyone was soaked to the skin in a very short time. But were dry again in just as quick a fashion, and turning around to have a last look while our feet were still on that Colón soil and as we climbed the gangway perhaps never to see that port again, but time will tell about all those things.

Early the next morning, the liner slipped her moorings and made her way through the wonderful lakes that were the beginning of the Panama Canal. Most of us had been up, and on leaving Colón had given them a great cheer, we did not intend missing seeing any of the Canal. We had heard all about the grand lochs, the settlements and plantations, the green wooded hillsides and jungle. Everything was as exciting and thrilling as was a new toy to a child. Small coloured children were playing about the banks of the Canal and now and again we were lucky enough to see the dangerous, notorious crocodile slipping through the mud. The sun was very hot and most everybody was dressed in shorts and a pair of sandals, reading for the present was forgotten, all eyes were turned to the slowly moving scenery.

It really was worth staying in the sun, for when the day drew to a close, the Canal began to come to its end and right before us we saw the great rollers of the blue Pacific. This again was a sight in a million, the golden sands and green jungle made a perfect setting for the lovely Pacific. We made our way to the channels at the mouth of the Canal, then got up a little more speed to bear us away nearer and nearer to our destination, Australia!

The Pacific side of America is very much better than the west, I thought. My main reason, I guess, was because we had left part of it to the cold weather of winter, while from here on it all seemed to be lovely sunny weather. This of course is really the best coastline in the USA. Anyway, we soon left it all behind and were once again in the blue solitude of sky and sea. Passing through the Panama gave us time to fill the pool because of it being fresh water, but was not for the use of swimming as the daily orders foretold but was to be used for washing clothing. No one liked the idea at first but as time went by we all found need for the water in the bathing pool. We each had quite a time at washing our gear here, in the brilliant sunshine, clad only in the usual shorts and sandals, everyone was getting sunburnt and I was sorry to say at that time I always went a bright red. It lasted a few months, then took the only other course and I went a light brown. We used to sit for hours in that sun with our washing. I often wondered, what would the folks back home say if they saw us half of the time? Anyway, time just stood still while we cruised around the Pacific, every now and again catching sight of some quaint tropical island with the familiar lines of waving palm trees, but these were some of the lucky ones where the war machine had not already looted and plundered. Maybe their turn would come? Let's hope not. The sights that were to follow have been told scores of times before, but only once from me, in these pages and here it will be the last time. Our voyage to Australia was coming to a rapid close and we only had about a week left aboard the liner *Dominion Monarch* and we would set foot on the much-discussed Australian soil. We wondered how the people lived, how they talked, and what fun they enjoyed the most, that was where I took the most notice. Swimming was everyday life to the Australian and it was also my favourite pastime. I knew I would love this country before I even set eyes on it.

You could feel the sense of approaching land and new adventure days before we saw land, but we kept about our daily toils and always made ready for a sudden landing if we got in ahead of time. The date of arrival was fixed for February 19th, three days ahead, but it was on the 22nd that we did arrive. The weather around these waters was very challenging because in Australia it was almost autumn and the rain began to get in our way a little but the sun was still quite warm. Anyway, the last week was in fact a very busy one, getting everything ready for leaving the ship and when the final day arrived, we were greeted by the best thunderstorm I have ever seen. The coast of Australia was looking very grim and grey with vivid flashes of lightning and sheets of rain, but we got through the middle of the heads of Sydney Harbour and moored in mid stream until the next morning. The buildings were just to be seen through the rain and to keep us company on our first evening in Sydney was the thunder and lightning.

GOLDEN HIND

We strolled the decks that same evening until the continuous downpour got most of us a little chilled. It was a real rough night with all the rain and thunder, tall buildings with their silhouettes standing out against the dark stormy sky after every flash of lightning, I thought it would never stop even when I was in my bed. I thought of a dark, wet morning and the last thing I heard that night was the patter of the raindrops on the porthole and the usual flash and the rumbles of a very thundery night.

To wake on the morning of February 22nd was like being at home in mid summer, it did not seem possible that after a night such as we had that there could be a grand morning, everything was so fresh and the sun was shining from a clear sky. We were all ready to leave the ship long before the first lads went, but we waited along the decks until our turn came. A band was playing along the quay and everywhere had an exciting atmosphere. People rushing around, welcoming our ship and the lads to Australia. The boat trains were already waiting for each section of the ship as we came ashore, some of the lads I knew had just managed to catch the train before mine. It was very warm carrying our kit about the platform, here, there and everywhere. Most of the large baggage had been stored away in the ship's hold, we would see that again when everything had been unloaded from the Liner and sent on the truck to our barracks, Golden Hind, about forty-five minutes from Sydney by train. The dock hands were having a front seat view of everything that was going on, they too thought it a little warm for work. Waiting there in the boiling sun was nice in a way, making a change from our winter at home. Our train was ready to begin the journey at last, after our smaller things had been loaded on and with a sigh of relief, we sat in the cool of the compartment taking in the view to be had from the window of the carriage. One thing that struck me, which had never been in our English trains, were the water jug and glasses in portable holders from each side of the compartment. These were soon put into use and again the lads on this train were thinking of what life had in store for them.

The houses, streets and parks that flashed by were so different from the usual ones of England. Houses were one storey and not quite so heavy and dull looking as at home, the streets did not seem to fall on each other as they have the habit of doing in most English towns, and the wide-open spaces were a real joy to behold. To think of all this space in English towns was but a dream, but of course that is getting off the beaten track. We stopped once or twice for signal lights and crossings and were delighted to find how the people were welcoming us along our way. From every house window was a kindly face calling out, 'How do, Cobber', 'Welcome, Bluey', 'Fair Dinkum'. It was great for a crowd of young lads so far away from home. Then we would be on our way again with the signal man waving his brake cloth which he used in his work with the points and catch point levers in his box. At one of these stops, a crowd of young boys got up onto the tracks and were asking for a few English coins. The dialogue of these small lads made quite a few smiles come to our faces such as, 'Gee, Mister, can ya spare a few coppers for us johnnies?' And, 'Whack ho, I got a real English penny,' with a very big drawing on the word penny. Most of them were quite happy-looking and well-built as were most of the Australian people that were to be found out by quite a number of lads that were sent back into the city to work. At last, we were really on our way and without any more hold-ups, we reached our new home that was to be ours for quite a time to come.

One of my pals was lucky enough to be put in the same tent as me. Of course the tents were just ideal for this weather, but were only in use until the real barracks were completed. Until then, we were to be housed in the middle of a racetrack that had been closed down for our comfort, trails were still kept handy for a little training and in the early hours of the morning you could see the horses being put through their paces. Pals always like to be together so Frank and I were thinking ourselves lucky to be in the same tent, and as luck would have it, we were to be together through quite a lot. Between one thing and another, looking forward to getting settled, and waiting for our first day ashore, our kits were dumped at the end stand — and what a pile! Hundreds upon hundreds of bags and hammocks. We were still looking for ours when night came and there is not much of a warning. Only the sun sinking in the west tells you in a few minutes it will be dark, of course to help things along it began to rain again. The grandstand was quickly made use of and some of the kit bags were left to the mercy of the rain, which as in

England was WET! Mine must have been the first to come out of the ship because I was one of the last to find mine, but it was dry and in one piece when I did find it. Frank was half asleep when I found my way to the tent. He had found his belongings hours before and all the pity I got from him was his remark, something about 'Picking up my bed and walking at this time of night.' It all came out in the wash as the old saying goes and after a few days had passed, we were ready for that first day ashore.

If I can remember rightly, it was on the Thursday when we first had our day off. February 26th or thereabout. We had been on Australian soil about one week. Frank and I were looking forward to this evening out and we were going to make the best of it, we always had our own train at the race course station waiting for us as we left so there was no rush and scramble to be first to get a seat. Everybody got a seat to himself; these trains were almost like our London subway trains and travelled at a very great speed. I always enjoyed these trips into the city; they always reminded me of a poem I learnt at school, which I have completely forgotten. A few words I do remember of it, one to quote, 'Faster than houses, hedges, ditches and faster than horses, broomsticks and witches,' the words might not be exact but that was the idea. The City of Sydney soon came into view and we were caught up in its great and lovely streets. A great feature was every soda fountain and milk bar, chocolate and sweets, fruit as cheap as dirt, that was my idea of it all and we made ourselves quite ill by the time we had finished. All the people were kind and helpful, we were treated as if we were kings and the costumes of the people were up to date. The girls knew how to dress alright, and could take their place among any girls in the world.

Looking around Sydney was very thirsty work, so we called in at one of the hotels in George Street, ordered a glass of wine and hoped for the best. The bill was much to my surprise — only six pence and a wine glass full. What a life! Anybody could get well away on 2/6 but we could skip that, we do not care to get involved in an essay on 'Law and Order' which is right up to the mark in Australian cities. If a person has had too much of it, it's best not to show it or otherwise drink yourself sober (nice death if you can manage it every night).

Frank and I did not get to those extremes but still had a very nice time. We caught the midnight train back to the barracks to contemplate on our weekend off when we had planned a great time. The weeks went by as if like magic and we got to like this land of sunshine very much. It was now March, and the swimming season was over. The summer time started about October and if the weather was found to be hot when we arrived, we were to find out how hot it really could get, but still we were able to stand the next summer in Australia because we met the hot climates halfway before the winter was over in Sydney. Although we never knew it then, two months after arriving, we found ourselves bound for the heart of the Philippine Islands. On the particular weekend that we were to embark on our Jap-infested waters, Frank and I were getting plans for a trip by tram along the city and getting out where we pleased. We carried out our plan and were never sorry for it, even today I still thank my lucky stars for the tram we happened to pick and the events that followed. This last week was spent in carrying out orders, draft routine, doctors and signing everything that we needed to allow us to enter the tropic waters of the North Pacific. All our things were ready to be carried off to our new ship and then the big event came — the name of our ship. It came as a surprise to me because after being the member of one carrier I thought I would be getting a change, but here again I was to be drafted to an aircraft carrier, and also the much-talked-about one too! HMS *Illustrious*. The ship that the Japs had claimed to have sunk three or four times before, but was still carrying on the fight with the enemy. She had only just returned from a rough sailing elsewhere on the globe but all that never came into my story, so therefore it can be told by people who took part and showed the dangers that go with a Pacific sea and air battle.

We left Golden Hind on the weekend we were supposed to take our tram ride and with the drafting from barracks to the ship, most of the time soon slipped away right until the Monday. The Friday evening that we left Golden Hind was not too kind to us, there had been quite a number of sharp showers, and of course before we could get the kit on board we were again caught in the sudden rain storms. We were working late into the evening, with the rain finding its way down the neck and under the oil skins, up the sleeves when we loaded the crane with our kit bags and hammocks until we were all feeling very much depressed, and to top everything off we were given orders to load the ship's fresh food supplies and spare parts, not forgetting the ammunition for guns and planes. Saturday dawned just after we retired.

HMS ILLUSTRIOUS

Our first real look at the *Illustrious* came with the Saturday morning routine, we were taken here, there and everywhere. The Master at Arms had his office around mid-ship, just near the upper-deck gangway and here were we to be given our mess numbers, part of the ship, Battle and Cruising Stations. Frank and I still stuck close together and we were delighted to find we were in the same mess and in the same Watch. Each ship had its own Watches, we called these by different colouring, such as Red Watch, White Watch, Blue Watch. Frank and I being in the Blue Watch, each one 'at sea' took over their respective watches, and which every man had to keep his eye on, trying not to miss your times of duty or you would surely be in for it. Everything depended on what time the ship sailed to state which watch went first and the watch that was on last. From the voyage before, we were the last to go on at the next sailing date. If Red finished up on the last trip, White would begin the next trip, so the routine would carry on. Our, what we called 'Duty Watch' had to be carried out on these lines. At sea it became all different named watches, around the clock, taking it from noon until noon the following day and they were — afternoon watch from 12.30 pm until 4 pm, the 'First Dog' 4 pm until 6 pm, 'Last Dog' from 6 pm until 8 pm, 'First Watch' 8 pm until midnight (eight bells), 'Middle Watch' midnight until 4 am (low bells) and 'Morning Watch' from 4 am until 8 am (eight bells). The fore noon watch completed the twenty four hours and had the longest number of hours from 8 am until 12.30 pm, so life and time went on around the clock. But Duty Watch in harbours meant one part of the watch took duty the whole of the day and the next one took its place leaving you 'The Stand-by Watch'. The name spoke for itself, the third watch took the second's place, leaving the first one 'Watch Ashore' which gave each watch one day out of the three ashore. Action Stations changed the whole outlook because everyone had an action station and had to drop whatever they were doing and they had to simply fly to their appointed station.

I was on the port side pom-pom (P-2) and amid ships on the flight deck. Frank was on the opposite side of me, on the starboard side in the Island pom-pom (S-4). The Island was the upper structure on the flight deck, the nerve centre of the carrier where the planes got their orders for taking off and all other instructions. Cruising stations were vice versa for Frank and I; we could always look across at each other whenever we thought it necessary. All the time we were aboard the *Illustrious*, we kept watch over each other and after each 'All Clear' we both looked over and smiled and thumbed up.

Our weekend was to be this very same one as we arrived aboard the carrier and therefore we made up our minds to take the tram trip from the city and out among the other parts of Sydney. We had of course been to the soda fountain bars and had had our fill of ice cream and all the nice things that go with it. The bars closed for two hours from 4 pm till 6 pm. We made use of the usual glass of wine at six pence, which to this day I still can't get over, and finally we caught a tram which was marked 'Rosebery'. We were again on an unknown adventure of our own. We rumbled and tumbled along leaving the centre and the main streets of the city behind, through unknown quarters and long avenues of palms, this was leading us further afield all the while so just as we were going to jump off we could see very bright lights, a lot of people and dance music coming from a distance up the street. We waited until we passed the spot and found it to be the small town hall dance of Waterloo, one of the many suburbs of the city. We alighted at the very next stop and made our way to the hall, it sounded very much as if the folks were having a wonderful time, so we went in. The chap at the door gave us a great welcome, trying to get us talking about everything at once, they were very kind to us and gave Frank and myself a great welcome. It took us almost half an hour to get to the floor, everyone seemed to be trying to welcome us in turn but at last we found our way in and beheld a very nice dance floor with a fairly good band playing the numbers I seemed to like best. We were really on show that evening, but we did not mind that is was not every day. British sailors found their way into Waterloo Town Hall without being invited. It was a family affair and just right to make ourselves at home. We danced with quite a number of the girls, that is what we went for of course, and spent a lot of time talking to the older folks who had left England mostly after World War One. It was very nice to be made to feel so at home by these warm and kind-hearted people. The evening wore on and just before the dance got down to its closing numbers, a middle-aged lady came over to us and sat down with the words, 'Sorry to keep you from dancing lads but I have been watching you two most of the evening and so has my daughter and her girlfriend. They have been longing to meet you but you have been too busy dancing to look over and see us.' She was English and had come out a number of years ago, very nice and homely, I say homely because we were both to see very much more of this family in the future. Their name was Reid and the daughter's name was Jean. The mother called Jean and her friend over, we were introduced and soon became friends. We were invited to have supper with them at their home, Mr Reid made an appearance and we became one big happy family. We had a few more dances and after meeting another friend of Mrs Reid's who asked us to dinner one weekend which we later accepted, we all left the hall for the Reid home, just around the corner. Jean had two other sisters and a brother who were all married and whom we met later on. This very kind family were really grand people to Frank and me; we were made to feel at home and were taken in as one of the family.

A family I shall never forget. This chance evening had given Frank and me something to treasure all our lives and the months that passed while we were out on the high seas. Mail and parcels got through to us from Jean, she was the most lovely and kind-hearted girl I had ever met. We all had quite a lot of fun at the house, we made them laugh with our sayings and they in turn made us laugh with the customs of an Australian family. I often think of the Reids, and someday I will return to visit them. That of course belongs in another story and is now among my doings of the past, it was a great pity we were to leave on the Monday morning but we arranged to write as often as we could and as soon as we came back from our operation somewhere in the Pacific we would get back to Waterloo as soon as we could manage the time off. Anyway, we left the Reids that evening after we had said goodbye about a hundred times. The tram stop was only across the street and Jean came with us to see us off. While we waited, each of us found it hard to make conversation, perhaps we were a little upset and did not want to leave so soon. Anyhow, the arrival of the tram saved the day and with a hurried handshake we left Jean waving us goodbye. We did not know when we would see her or her family again. Of course, we had their address and could write as often as we could. A few months would pass before we really did see Jean again, but it seemed like it was years that rolled and rolled around.

We reached the city in a few minutes and walked the rest of the way to the ship. The air was grand, the summer was almost at an end and after a few showers in the day the evening was good, but now the cooler weather was coming, we were off to parts much warmer. Most people on board were already retired for the night because of the large amount of work which had to be done before we were due to sail on the morning tide and we hoped everything was ready for us to leave on time. We did sail on time as it happened. To return to Sydney!

HMS Comet at sea from Hong Kong to Australia 1946. Author is 2nd row from bottom and 2nd from right.

HMS Illustrious Captain Cook Dock Sydney Harbour 1945

Roof of Bank of Sydney at Martin Place 1946
Rogers, Cole, Wilson and Jarvis

On board the HMS Furious 1944
Top row: Maquire & Haynes
Bottom row Rogers & Brown.

Mishap on deck on the Illustrious 1945 Okinawa raids

HMS Furious. Author is top row, 2nd from the right

HMS Furious in Norway 1944

Japanese suicide attack on the Illustrious 6/4/45

Ship's company HMS Comet June 1946

HMS Comet Hong Kong 1946

HMS Comet 1946 Fremantle W.A.

USN Saratoga taken from the HMS Illustrious

6 May 1944 Members of the crew of the Furious have an early breakfast of ham sandwiches and cocoa during the operation against the Bismark. Note the pom poms.

His Majesty the King visits the fleet in northern waters August 1941 on board ships of the home fleet.

PACIFIC WARFARE

We left Sydney at dawn, with the sky a blaze of colour, and the air so still I wondered what the folks at home would be doing at the moment, perhaps they too were thinking of me across the other side of the world. I always tried to put as much as I can into my letters about my life and what I have been doing and I hoped they didn't worry about me too much. The chief of course was always on our heels making sure we kept a tight lip about the whereabouts of our ship and others of the South Pacific Fleet. Sometimes it was hard to keep back the most important parts of our letters, but we knew well enough that it would be folly to break our silent service rules. All of this came to my mind as we sailed through Sydney Heads and out towards the open sea. We passed lovely houses with their private beaches, boat moorings, and swimming pools all looking beautiful in the early morning light. I took a last look towards the city before it was lost behind the rocks and cliffs of the coastline and wished that I could come back to Australia and Sydney again to these loving and friendly people. I was not on watch until the afternoon, 12.30 pm, so we were still off duty for a while. The weather was in our favour that morning, the sea which is always rough and angry was calm and almost as smooth as glass and the breeze that managed to creep up was hardly noticeable, in the old sailing days such weather would no doubt be very unwelcome but I seemed to glory in it. No falling from one side to the other with the motion of the ship. There was no swell that morning and that helped to give us a little heart after leaving Australia because from now on we knew we had to all fight and pull together. Everybody was in the same boat, so to speak.

Australia had been left far behind and as is custom on board an RN ship, the Captain spoke on the loudspeaker about our future plans and destination which were to be in and around the Admiralty Islands and then the Philippines and Samoa. This was going to prove quite busy and the Japanese were really keen to get rid of us all. The carriers were in constant danger of the notorious suicide planes so we were always at the ready for these 'little devils' and as things turned out all our ships and planes were in turn attacked by these 'Honour by Death' men, diving and blasting wherever they happened to crash. Anyway, all this comes in its turn, as I said a little while ago, we were heading to the Admiralty Islands and this was to be our base, and proved to be a great help in the weeks that were to follow. We had settled in on our new ship with ease and like it or not was very good. The *Illustrious* was a grand carrier and had plenty of space to walk about. The time for my afternoon watch was slowly approaching and as I mentioned earlier, we were on 'cruising stations'. Whenever the fleet was not otherwise engaged in action it was called 'cruising stations'. As the lunch hour arrived, it was served in the mess hall and the rum was issued out and everyone took 'sippers' which meant being given a spot of rum from one of the lads, because some of us were not old enough for drawing our tot and on our twenty-first birthday we were allowed to draw our first rum and that was how it was in those days.

My tot was still awaiting my coming of age, the age that counts anyway. The twenty-first birthday was a great thing to the young chaps.

Anyway, lunch was over and we were quite ready to go up on watch, it would have been quite nice up there on deck in the sunshine, heading for the Coral Sea and then New Guinea. Sailing away on the ocean was and still is to me a grand sensation. These waters seemed to hold a spell of their own. The rise and fall of the swell seemed to meet at the right moment with the distant horizon. The sky was always of the deepest blue, and even before a storm, you had the feeling of it being just the right colour for a lovely day. While on our cruising watch we had plenty of time to look out over the sea and let our imagination run away with us. The war seemed so far away at times like these, it was so peaceful. But coming back to earth again, one could easily see the other ships of war riding the waves. Seeing other carriers with their planes at the ready on the flight deck, reaching with their wings and props into the empty space, we knew they would take off somewhere and never return, taking their pilots and crew to a watery grave. Others were lucky enough to return to their carriers safely only to take off over and over again, fighting against great odds and wondering if the ship would be in one piece when the flight returned as the sudden attacks by the Japanese and the suicide planes were trying to destroy one ship or the other.

The pom-pom gun was in the shade of the bridge portside and was my place for action stations, I could see the other pom-pom from where I was and one of my pals was at his pom-pom and we could see each other if we looked over the gun shelf, it proved to be a very good way for finding out how we were getting on after the coming of some 'hot water'. He was on watch the same time as I was. Everything could be seen that was of interest as we sailed along. There were small islands in the distance and others that looked like you could almost touch them with your hands. The bow of the ship seemed to touch the island with the rough cliffs and waving palms but no sign of life anywhere and knowing only too well there may be eyes watching the strange ships sailing by. The Japs could most likely be hiding there as well, but we could not be sure of this, anyway we did not trouble to stop and find out. Our orders were to get to the Admiralty Islands where we would find all the Japs we needed. The lads were always full of life while on watch, finding something of interest to talk about and it would be mostly about the shores of England.

Very few ever got tired of talking about home and when they got back home hoping things would be just right for the service boys and girls. The debt England owed to these people could never be repaid, but all we were thinking of down the war years, was freedom and a place of one's own in a new world. What would be in store for each and every one of us after all this was over?

Time fled by in these pleasant surroundings of sea and sky and while we talked and dreamed, others took our place waiting with the weapons of war. Day after day went by until we reached the islands that were to be our base for many a month and a shelter while we would refuel and take our rest.

These islands were very welcome to the fleet, the air strip seemed to jut out from the very waters, the earth was very low in parts and one had the impression that planes and the palms were just reaching out of the blue waters. The golden sands and the deep green of the jungle was a just a grand sight for a lad seeing all this for the first time as never before getting very far beyond our own shores. Everything seemed to be just wonderful when seeing them for that first great moment. The contrast from these shores to the coast of Norway was worth their weight in gold. In Norway, you felt the ice in the wind, and hail and snow and clouds that seemed to find their way into every nook and corner of the rocks and snow-filled hills, and out here among the lovely warm rays of the sun and soft warm waters lapping the beaches and the breeze rustling through the trees and palms of the dense jungle. I am not quite sure what we expected for our base and anyway we would be too busy to think much about it. Our main concern of course was that it was a handy place to refuel and replace spent ammunition and also good protection from any snooping and low-flying enemy planes and the base was near enough to the Philippines and beyond this the islands of Japan where we were to spend just as much time as we could manage. And so, while all the crazy world was fed up to the neck with the war we sailed into the bay of our Pacific Base. We stayed here long enough to find out what folk meant about hot and stuffy weather, we were feeling it more than usual because of our just sailing through the Coral sea with plenty of breeze and thin air and now being sheltered in the bay by the jungle and on all sides sloping sand dunes, and now after a short stay here preparing for a Pacific war, we had begun to get a little bored and as regards to the actual warfare for all we knew if may have ended.

We had not seen any real fighting since the Germans gave us

not a moments rest all over the North Sea, between their bombing our convoys and playing hide and seek with the pocket battle ship *Tirpitz* then the ever-present attempt to save lads of both sides, trapped pilots from the shot-up planes that were doomed when they crashed into the icy North Sea and more than fifty percent of the pilots were frozen to death before help could arrive, but those cold days only seemed to be a bad dream while we complained of the heat and the quiet hush of the jungle where we hoped to find ample Japs to finish off amid the glory of a hundred and one sea battles we only find the peace and quiet of an English village in midsummer, we were not thinking then of course of our many months ahead among these islands. Japan was still very much on her toes and we were soon to forget the nonsense of being left out of the war, if we had really known what part some of us would have to play before the war was over most of us would be really troubled no doubt; I was lucky, a number of my mates on our company carriers were heading for a night move and for a few. it ended in death and wounds that would leave them marked for life. The climate may soon very well change out in the tropical seas and as soon as we left the Admiralty Islands the winds were much cooler and made things easier to get about one's work and while on watch on the pom-pom on the flight deck the cool breezes were very welcome and most of our time off was also spent there talking and laying in the sun.

In one of the lift wells which were used for carrying the planes from the hangars to the flight deck, we had a huge canvas swimming pool where everyone had the time of their lives and it was only used in harbour in non-dangerous waters. In harbour, the best swimming was done over the side though, the Duty

Officer and boat's crew were always at the ready in case one was foolish enough to try to swim too far from the ship and get himself into difficulties and also to watch for any hidden dangers that may be lurking in the depth of these waters of the Pacific. Those few moments in the canvas swimming pool did most of us the world of good. The water was pumped from the sea and it really was salty, if anybody happened to be in a playing mood the victim was in the water before he knew what was happening and to help the laughter on, someone also got a mouthful of very salty water and a nice eye bath, but it is all in the fun of the day and so as each day passed someone or other got this 'joke in the neck'. Life at sea could become quite monotonous and a good motto of mine was 'laugh and grow fat'. Most of my spare evenings after I came off watch while we were at sea would be to sit in the foremost part of the flight deck with my mate whom I shall call Ted, as I used this name while we were on our first visit to Sydney.

The flight deck was a very cool place at night. The breeze caused by the speed of the ship was smashing. It rushed up over the bow and over the flight deck where we sat and many others had the very same idea and in their usual high spirits we always had a nice time. The duty watch men were forever at their posts and my next watch would be the next day, so I could enjoy the cool breeze until late into the night sitting amongst the cables and the anchors. On the edge of the flight deck you got the feeling of flying just above the surface of the sea watching the distant horizon getting closer but never showing it and with the other ships behind us, everything felt so strange, the wide open space of ocean and sky but the tell-tale wake of the ship as we ploughed through the sea was always a great danger at night, as the propellers stirred up the sea into a white foam which could be seen for a great distance behind the ship. An enemy pilot smart enough to notice this could soon bring about some trouble to spoil a nice cool enchanting evening off.

Writing mail was still my best hobby and I did quite a lot of it. Jean back in Australia wrote often to Ted and me and we always received a letter each and when we wrote back we always used to kid her about each other, poor Jean would always tell each of us off in turn when we were all back in Australia again. We spent many hours laughing at the whole affair. Most of these good times were grand to look back on but many a night I would be on watch and think of other times that were not too good. One of them was when I was aboard my first aircraft carrier, *Furious*, a good old ship which will live long in my memory, it was tempting fate for me, but it never failed to bring a smile to my face. It happened as I was getting ready for my 'middle watch', my mate from the gun crew had given me a shake and was at the job of giving the other unlucky souls a shaking. Myself not feeling too good, getting up at midnight, was only half awake and not thinking where I had slung my hammock, which as misfortune would have it was right above the cable house pipe, this being the passageway from the cable deck for the lowering of the anchor sling when the ship is moored, my very tired feet and body dropped from the hammock, not upon the deck as my half-alert mind thought them to be, but upon the damp slippery cable and anchor, which were always at the ready to be cut away at a moment's notice. Upon alighting none-to-gently on the cable, I at once lost my balance, but not before I let out a blood-freezing yelp and down I went to what I thought was going to be a very wet grave. I managed to fall part of the way, but at last the anchor gave no room for me to pass so there I came to rest, the sea rushing against the bow and spray playing about my face and ill-clad body — not a very comforting position to be in. I was very lucky not to have been crushed and to have found my way beyond the anchor to the sea. As I said before, this mishap came into being as a lot of the crew were coming off watch, so I had quite a number of rescuers about. There were flashing lights, yelling and shouting, all rushing to save a life or save a body. Within a few minutes I was panting upon the deck; how hard and wonderful it felt.

Of course I was dazed, bruised and shaking like a leaf and almost about to burst into tears if I remember rightly, but still I wondered how many people had been jammed between an anchor and the house pipe and were any second likely to drop into the cruel sea and out of existence at the age of eighteen. My watch was still to go ahead so I managed to dress as best as I could, scramble along the cable deck through the mess decks and up among the planes on the flight deck. By the time I got to my gun, everybody was on watch, the leading hand wanting me to know what the hell did I think this was, a tea party? I managed to mumble, 'Sorry' and fell across the foot plate, must have gone a little dizzy walking across from the cable. Not until then did he notice there was something wrong, I had begun to shake again and my poor bruises were hurting like the devil, must have cracked my head as well, as I had dried blood on my forehead. A word to the Officer of the Watch and I was sent back to my hammock for a good night's rest — but not before I moved to a more protective place. I did not want to tempt fate for a second time. It took me quite a little time to get over that but everybody was good about it, they forgot it ever took place. Not like most mid-ships when you have your leg pulled for ages afterwards. My little accident was too new for that.

Thoughts good and bad came to mind, like that on a lonely watch we each took a turn on the earphones in case of messages from the control when on cruising stations, and the warm tropical evenings lead me to thinking of events that took place so much nearer to home. Our quiet and easy voyage had begun to be taken for granted. Our only contact with war these days were the ships we sailed. Cruising stations came and went without mishap, the ship's company getting very suntanned and feeling full of cheer. Our night-long watches began to take on a feeling among the men of wasted time, but how little we knew then as we sailed peacefully towards the Philippines and the new kind of warfare to what we had been used to in other parts of the globe and as we sailed nearer to our goal, things on board carried on as they had been doing since leaving South America and the Panama Canal, but of course those days sailing out from England were the better days of our naval careers and we were about to embark upon the real dangers of the so-much-talked-about beautiful Pacific of the pre-war days. The whole of the ship's company was right up to the mark with duties and efficiency, all action stations were known by every officer and rating.

Cruising stations were just as important, everything done on board ship is important, some men found out the hard way, some found out by paying with their lives, the rules to know quite a lot about is the importance of being earnest. The fleet were quite on their mark as we sailed through the magic waters of the South

Seas, everyday life was carrying on as usual. The other ships looked harmless and friendly in the warm sunshine, but night brought a veil of extra precaution and tense waiting by the watch on duty.   Everyone knew we were not in waters that were altogether safe to be sailing in. The Japs were in existence in the waters we were using and without anyone saying such, the atmosphere of waiting was felt in every part of the vessel. Waiting can be one of man's worse enemies.

The raids on the Japanese-held islands were about to commence and after so long in preparing for it, the plane crews were being put through their paces again. They were a fine bunch of lads and every time they flew from the ship, their lives were in their own skill and daring and in combat with Japs, fighting was much different, the chief things in the mind of every Jap was to die for their God and the Rising Sun!

We had been doing these 'search convoys' for quite some weeks and had begun to get used to Jap cunning. Our main job was to destroy or cripple enemy bases and strongholds that were dotted about the islands, these bases enabled the Japs to re-arm planes and re-fuel ships among other things useful to them for their endless attacks upon our supply ships and cargo for the allies.

We were all sitting around the mess table talking and waiting for our 'watch' to be due to start and be at our posts, the lads on watch at that moment had a few scares through their few hours on action stations as Jap subs had been picked up by our radar and this meant we were being watched and under threat of air attacks by the infamous suicide bombers. The submarines would inform them of our whereabouts and with thoughts of action in the near future, our watch relieved the other lads. The weather was rather warm these days, sailing along the quiet ocean, and the ship's crew were content to let the time slip by trying to keep the thoughts of war away, talking instead of the girlfriends and pals left behind in Australia. Nobby would always have a cheery word to say as I took my position on the gun. This particular day, I had hardly climbed over the rail from the deck to the gun platform when he smiled and said, 'Another watch for day-dreaming Red, we seem to have the white dove of peace with us this trip.'

I grinned and said as straight faced as I could 'Don't tell me you still have that crush on the blonde at Kings Cross?'

My answer was a swiping from the ammo chamber across the side of the head and before I could return the volley of attack, the gun's captain blared out, 'Guns crew close up, practice run, zero to seventy five percent, so on, so on.' A refresher run keeps even the best crew on their toes. Half the watch over, we were all getting bored as usual, some laying about gazing out to sea following the rest of the convoy with a sweeping eye, others writing down a few lines to the folks and friends at home, everything going along as normal, at least for the next few minutes then before we had time to count to ten, everything around us became a scene of sudden death. A few planes had suddenly appeared over the horizon without warning, were headed straight towards us and then climbed high into the air and fell in the midst of the convoy. Our guns roared into life and we found the Japs already keeping well out of the range of our guns, the first plane had attempted to crash upon one of the carrier's decks but must have misjudged the death dive or perhaps one of the ships had found its target in record time, the main thing was the first plane was out of action.

There were still two more to go though and from my gun I could see the outer range of ships putting up a fight to claim a prize, the zooming and crashing of guns were in constant demand but the two planes continued to try for a clear passage to death and destruction. The carnage continued for many more minutes. Jap planes roared high in the air to suddenly swoop down to find their next target in their suicide dives. I was spellbound at the Japanese suicide pilots and their intention to give their lives to their so-called Gods or country or whichever it was. I was soon awakened from my view of destruction by shouts and screams from my gun mates. 'The bastards have got us in their sights!' Lofty screamed. 'Train the guns for God's sake!' the orders rebounded. I saw the plane turn sharply and head for us. Straight for me, I knew it. Down he came. I actually saw that grinning face seconds before he crashed inches from the ship's side. The crash and shower of wake was horrific. We got the deluge of water and a flag of the rising sun. I was breathless as I stared through the dripping water at the continuing attacks of the death dives. A huge explosion aft told us the ship must have been hit. God have mercy, I thought, have any of the lads been killed? Is the damage serious? 'To hell with the enemy!' I yelled.

The raid of intended carnage was over. I took a quick glance at the fleet, to the sight things looked presumably alright. At the end of our watch we retired to our mess decks, waiting for news of the damage to our aircraft carrier. The time dragged on until it became a nightmare and that nightmare became reality in the form of a damaged propeller. That was good news of a sort, at least no fear of anyone being killed or injured. The result of course was a return to base for repairs.

Return we did, our destination was the Captain Cook dry dock in Sydney at Woolloomooloo. This trip eventually happened, and we spent time at ease, but for me the long-term news was not so rosy. Orders were that the *Illustrious* was to return to England and some of us on board had not qualified for our foreign service so had to go back to the barracks in Sydney named Golden Hind at Warwick Farm, a suburb a little way out of Sydney. I left *Illustrious* in May 1945 and stayed at the Golden Hind until late May that same year.

IOMP

From there, I was assigned to the Staff Flag Officer Naval Air Pacific.

My having to leave the HMS *Illustrious* was a very sad blow. I had enjoyed my stay as a member of the crew through thick and thin. The times of battle with the Japanese suicide planes would forever mar my memory. I often thought many, many times about whether these young men were very brave or to my mind, brainwashed, but there it was, there was a parting of the ways for me. I really did leave the *Illustrious* with a very heavy heart, having not completed my foreign service time it was a very bitter cross to bear, seeing the *Illustrious* for the last time would remain heavy in my heart forever. But leave I did, and my next port of call was at the Naval barracks at Warwick Farm. This had been a racetrack before the Navy took it over for our needs. There was a very handy railway line into the racetrack compound presumably for the race-going public. Getting a ride right into the ground was very handy for we lads coming back from shore leave. Here I was to stay until orders came through with news of my next draft chit. A short spell at Warwick Farm had me dreaming of the days when this place would be swarming with happy punters in the glorious Australian sunshine. The rows of huts and tents were lodged in the centre of the track. What a difference it would have been on carnival day. A racetrack can be very exciting, especially if you were on a winning streak. It was really pleasant just having to wait around for orders to embark on my next Navy adventure. In due course my assignment did arrive, I was to join the staff of the Flag Officer (Admiral Portal) Navy Air Pacific FONAP, but to my great surprise no ship was to come out of this. The Post was a bank building taken over by the Navy right in the heart of Sydney and not at all far from Sydney's famous bridge. My part in the staff of the Admiral was not a prodigious appointment but I was assigned to be a guard at the entrance to the building, wearing the necessary uniform of a guard, smart and neat and a cap at the very right angle. I was set for a fairly long stay at the Admiral's headquarters. There would be the usual naval watches and arriving at my billet was another surprise. There were a number of ratings on this assignment and we shared one of the top floors for our living quarters. Life in the city for a sailor was a pretty terrific life to have.

But here in the middle of the city, I met the other Navy rating who was to be my very best friend always. His name was Fred, the same as mine, his hometown in the UK was Torquay and mine was Pontypool in Wales. Fred and I took our new positions very well. We did have different watches to keep but there were days when we had shore leave together. These days proved to be delightful in many ways. We were able to scout the city together which helped a lot in a strange environment. A very pleasant sojourn was to the many beaches surrounding Sydney. Trams were always plentiful and all we had to do was dash onto the first available tram and away we would go to many destinations. This practice took us to many nice places, one beach in particular took our fancy. It was on the north side called Neilson's Park. It was really part of the huge harbour and to my way of thinking, a good place to avoid those nasty sharks. The park had a safety net to protect bathers from those terrors of the deep. Out in the middle of the swimming enclosure was a large pontoon where you could swim out to and get burnt to death by the hot rays of the sun and there was plenty of sunshine on our days off. The longest run if I remember rightly was to a beach called Palm Beach. It was a fair way from the city but once you got there it was quite nice. There was only a tiny shop there and an ancient small wharf landing, but Fred and I took the beach to our hearts and spent some great days laying in the sun — a practice I was to suffer from for years afterwards. We had great times also with the rest of the lads at headquarters. The Admiral had a WREN driver named Margaret; she was a very jolly girl. We used to reminisce on times about England and what the scars of war had dealt them. One day, Fred and I read about a dance to entertain the forces at a place named Ashfield. It was a suburb of Sydney and not too far out of the city. A few of us who had shore leave went off to Central Station and got a train to Ashfield, and low and behold Fred met the love of his life there. A beautiful girl named Sadie. She had friends with her, and we soon gathered up the conversation of first meetings. Tea and bikkies were in great demand and Fred and Sadie were never short of conversation. As the days passed into weeks and months, the romance between these two lucky people grew very strong. On another occasion at Ashfield, we were to meet a very elderly man who invited us to meet his family and as luck would have it, he lived in Frederick

Street. How was that for the powers of fate? His name was Mr Hall and meeting his family was a delight. A family I was to share part of my life with some years ahead. Also, invitations came from other families through the Red Cross and St Vincent's. One family visited me on a day's outing in their car. Fate struck me again as the couple's children whose names were Elsie and Archie Rogers. With this couple, I was to remain friends with until they departed this world.

Another family who were kind enough to invite me to their home was a Mr and Mrs Frazer living in the Blue Mountains, an hour or two from Sydney. They had a son and a daughter and by chance they also knew a son of Mr Hall who had a Gladiolus farm right there in Blackheath where the Frazer family lived. I got along with Mr Frazer's son, Clifford, extremely well, he had had a terrible accident with his horse whilst out riding. He had been kicked in the head and the result being a plate inserted, he seemed rather well in coping with this accident but some time later Clifford was to die from the ghastly happening. But in the meantime, I was to enjoy my stay with the Frazers and in years ahead I was privileged to have the Frazers at my wedding after my return to Australia after being demobbed, but that in itself would have to be another story. My times spent at Blackheath were very warmly experienced. Meanwhile, after getting back from short shore leave, the duties of the moment were always present. Fred and I spent many hours 'doing the town' but as the time passed, Fred was beginning to spend his off-duty hours at Croydon where Sadie lived with her family, who hailed from Scotland. Mr and Mrs Berry arrived in Australia many years before. If I remember rightly, I have an idea they came out to

Australia on a sailing ship, but never mind, they were there when we needed company so much. I don't think we ever got used to the weather in Australia being so kind to us. My first winter in Australia sailed through like a summer breeze. Mostly blue skies, happy people and a world apart from everything. But sadly, the war had to eventually strike at the heart of the nation. Bombs rained down on Darwin, the black cloak of death named the Jewel of the Pacific. The long hours on duty watch brought tales of the war on to my daydreaming. The war was at its lowest ebb. Japan had surrendered after that ghastly bomb was dropped. Even Hitler had come to his very-deserving end. My life at that moment was tranquil after my own experiences from 1943. The Rogers were kind enough to include me still in their outings. I saw a lot of the towns not too far away from Sydney, I also spent a lot of time with the Berry family and on those occasions, Fred would tell me he had positive notions of remaining in Australia for his demob. I really did not for one minute feel surprised. I knew very well Fred and Sadie were extremely close. How Sadie was pleased about Fred's intended actions was a sight to behold. The whole family was truly delighted; as for myself, romance was not too conflicting. I did meet on one occasion a very nice girl from the suburb of Waterloo, just outside Sydney. She lived with her mother in a nice moderate home and I did enjoy their company. There were dances and small gatherings, walks and window shopping, but never stopping to buy.

HMS COMET AND HONG KONG

Duty went on and on until the time came when the axe fell again. It was on February 3rd when I was told I had been assigned to HMS *Comet*. That was alright, the *Comet* I knew was not an aircraft carrier, the ships I had been used to, but nevertheless it was a means of getting on my way to the pending days of demob. The months towards the end of the Pacific would be dated for 1947. The only trouble I had in boarding the *Comet* was the fact that she was in Hong Kong harbour. That seemed a bit of a stumbling block, this was going to be a dandy of an operation, the Navy came to the rescue by plonking me on the Shropshire for a two-week cruise, but suddenly we had orders to turn back to Sydney. Off I went again to barracks for a further two weeks' leave. An unexpected signal and I was once more on my way, this time on HMS *Anson*. Leaving Sydney on April 10th, 1946. I found out our destination was Kure, Japan. We arrived there on April 24th, 1946. Life aboard a different ship proved to be somewhat of a challenge. Different officers and duties to be overseen by the officer of the day. On the whole, life remained fairly sweet and Japan was now not a place to be scared of, but low and behold my marching orders came again, or should I say I got my sailing into the sunset orders? This time, out of the blue came my next fly-by-night ship, this was to be the HMS *Vengeance*. Were there many ships left for me to board? I wondered. I had a stout heart and the will to take all things for granted, so climb aboard I did. At last I was on my way to Hong Kong. Sounds like a mariner's swan song!

Arriving in Hong Kong on April 30th, 1946 was a nice surprise because there was the HMS *Comet* laying off in the harbour in the brilliant sunshine, a much smaller ship than the *Furious*, much smaller indeed. Not a sighting of a flight deck either, she was just the *Comet* and it was love at first sight. A grey beauty resting in the busy turmoil of Hong Kong harbour, small vessels dotted everywhere. San pans with their families living aboard, I really didn't know how, and all the backdrop of modern Hong Kong of 1946. What a different atmosphere indeed. I could imagine putting the *Comet* on the flight deck of the *Illustrious*. Everything seemed in miniature. Mess deck, upper deck, distance from stern to bow, all needed to be checked but I could see without a doubt I was going to have trouble getting down to a much smaller existence and as I looked down from the ship's rail, I took in the sight of the harbour with wonder and a keen eye to notice a san pan resting in the water almost alongside. A very old looking man was on the deck staring up at me. I didn't know what it was, but I felt drawn to him for some reason, it really sent cold shivers up and down my spine. He had on one of those large, brimmed straw hats and was wearing a kind of loose cloak. He yelled up to me suddenly, 'You have red hair.' He wasn't far wrong there; it was a kind of red but my Navy documents told me my hair was auburn. His little boat was tossing about in the swell and I fancied he was trying to reach up to me. 'You come down on my boat or I climb up on your boat.' I gave a gasp of surprise, quickly glancing about me I saw no one to contact. I yelled down to him to say he couldn't climb aboard; it wasn't allowed but why do you need to come aboard? I asked. 'You have good fortune!' he called back and somehow to my amazement, he threw a grabbling line and there he was standing beside me.

Before I could recollect my thoughts, he had taken both my hands into his. For a second he stared down at my palms then he stared up into my eyes and smiled. All I could do was hold my breath. What the hell was I doing standing there holding hands with a Chinaman? I thought to myself.

'Very young boy to be away from home,' he whispered. 'You have long life,' he pointed to the lines on my palms. At once the penny dropped, he was something of a fortune teller. I tried to get away. What if one of the officers came up on deck and caught me being chummy with this bloke, I thought to myself very quickly.

'Young boy with red hair,' he repeated. 'You will live to be one hundred years old,' he added.

'Don't be daft,' I answered, trying to laugh but my throat felt too dry.

'You sail away on long voyage to meet love of life!'

Long voyage, we all knew that was true. Love of my life, that could be pending for a very long time to come. The next thing he said really did make me laugh. He told me I would be having three children in a land so big. If they are triplets, I'll come back to haunt you, I answered.

'You best get back down to your boat before my captain puts us both in the loony bin, mate,' I added in rather a harsh tone of voice. One of my mess mates suddenly appeared and he came up to me and asked why I looked green in the gills.

'He just came aboard,' I whispered.

'Who came aboard?' he remarked. I looked at him in amazement. I turned to face the Chinaman but he was gone. I glared down at his san pan and there he was as if he hadn't been standing alongside me on deck. I gave a sudden gulp.

'Don't tell me I've been daydreaming again,' I said aloud.

'You've been out in the sun too long, mate,' my fellow sailor said.

I simply left if at that and we began our way back along the deck, I dared not look down into the water for fear the Chinaman and his boat were not there. Sitting at the mess table, I wondered if the crack on the head falling down the hose pipe on the *Furious* could have made a problem with my stupid mind concerning my meeting with the so-called Chinese gentleman. Don't tell me I'm going round the bend? I must have spoken out loud, because my mate alongside me at the mess table gave me a dig in the ribs and wanted to know what I was yapping about. 'I'm off to the head,' I answered my mate and headed out. Suddenly I remembered someone saying we were off to Western Australia. That would be a huge slice of land as that was what the Chinaman spoke about. Hell's bells, I thought as I got to the head. I must be going nuts! Going back to Australia would be strange and fitting in with my supposed meeting with the man in the san pan and the announcement that I would be having three children later on. That suddenly made me laugh and I felt much better for it.

But life proved satisfactory and word from the captain via his officers one and all regarding orders, duties and the important act of protocol. I settled into the part of the ship that was going to be my home for as long as the axe refused to fall on my neck again. Time passed by. I had the good fortune to be aboard when the ship settled for a while in Repulse Bay. The time seemed to fly away and May was fast coming to an end. Sometimes nostalgia took over the reins and my mind went back to Fred and Sadie back there in Sydney. I wondered whether Fred had fared well with the admiralty concerning his demob occurring in Australia instead of his return to England. I took my mind's eye to the Blue Mountains and poor Clifford and his family. The Rogers family and our super trip in the car. The Hall family with their love of fruit salad and the day of sun and roses in their garden. The sentimental mind is worth its weight in gold. Many a time I was released of tension through long hours of duty watches. The stay in Repulse Bay came to an end. July had arrived and we were ordered to set sail again, but low and behold we were to return to Australia, but this time it was to the other side of this vast continent. Western Australia was on the charts. Coming back to Australia, well it seemed so strange after the voyaging I had done in the past month. Would I ever look back on the trips on so many ships, I wondered, and would there be more after the *Comet* that I would have to board scoring a berth to merry England?

Leaving Hong Kong seemed something of a relief, I don't know why but the thought of sailing away to Australia again appeared to me to be an omen. Was it because of Fred staying in Australia instead of going back to England? Did I want to return to England myself? Somehow the thought bothered me. I began to think of my own family if I remained in Australia. I didn't think I could really settle properly in Australia without first returning to stay with my family after all the years of being away. Another thought occurred to me, perhaps I could stay in England for a while then after a reasonable length of time return to Sydney to visit some dear friends. The glorious beaches beckoned me. The huge expanse of land intrigued me. What a wonderful thing it would be to travel all over Australia before settling down to a presumed married life. I would have to wait until my stretch in the Royal Navy was over and perhaps how I will fare in Western Australia. As usual I was awakened from my daydreaming by a buzz that we would be crossing the line after we did a stay in Tarakan, that being our first stop before calling in at Dili in Timor. Reaching the impending crossing-the-date-line in between these ports of call was something some of us aboard *Comet* had never had the chance of doing before. Entering this port of call at Tarakan was by no means very exciting. I spent quite a lot of time there on duty and catching up on writing mail. I seemed to have an abundance of letters to take care of new friends in Sydney deserved a letter or two after such warm welcomes. Folks at home of course were at the top of my list and with one thing and another we set sail in the sunset for Western Australia.

My heart seemed to miss a beat at the thought of once again being back in Australia, but things were stirring aboard ship. The Captain and his officers were busy doing what had to be done for the infamous crossing-of-the-date-line celebrations. The tradition of the line-crossing represented a rite of passage for sailors. The ceremony traditionally was overseen by someone who had already crossed the line and dressed up as King Neptune (ruler of the high seas). The ceremony brought us closer together and tightened up the crew. Many sailors remember their first line crossing as one of their most memorable experiences of their careers. When you come to think of it, there really was a lot of planning to get through. It was the equivalent to a well-staged pantomime. I imagine every sailor and officer would know of the skulduggery that goes on under the banner of merriment. Most of us have seen what goes on in other vessels who happen to cross the path of King Neptune in one form or other. Our crossing the line was not going to be far from upheaval. The crew of *Comet* were really a fun-loving lot of chaps and we were looking forward to the day when crossing the line came into being and was going to be a corker of a celebration. How long would we have to wait until the Captain approved of the timeless cast members was yet to be seen but under the cloak and dagger shield I knew everything was going according to plan.

The day eventually arrived by the supposed signal message from somewhere out there in the deep. I was busy with my duty watch routine when the word came about that the excitement was afoot. The beings of the deep had spied *Comet* getting very close to the infamous 'Line'. I caught a glance of the Captain in earnest conversation with his first officer, other officers appeared and also a few ratings. Methinks the Captain was getting his jolly band together for rehearsals. Then the beginning of a very happy experience came over the ship's loudspeaker. We were told a signal had been received from the creatures of the deep.

The passage from Tarakan had so far been quite un-disturbing except for the continuing talk about crossing the line. I just cannot explain how the atmosphere on behalf of the crew changed.

Every nook and cranny of the ship was alive with fun and frolic anticipation. Even the 'old salts' were akin to the promise of the goings-on of the crossing. I know for a fact the entire list of officers were to be included. At one time I was tempted to waylay my officer of my part of the ship and ask if there was any truth about collaring some of the ratings to be victims of the King of the Sea. The officer over me was Sub Lieutenant Richard Beaumont. The very honourable Sub Lieutenant Beaumont, but each time we were near enough for conversation some matter of the ship's duties came between us, it might have been just as well for all I knew he might have been mustered for the role of King Neptune himself. I let my haywire curiosity take care of itself. Instead, I went about my duties diligently, but I always kept my nose close to the grindstone, so to speak. Time passed by and the truth would come out in the end. All I had to do was twirl my thumbs, keep a close watch on the antics going on around me and everything in the garden would be rosy. But could I wait so long? Just as well, my part of the ship kept me busy until that moment.

REMINISCING ABOUT AN EVENT ON THE *FURIOUS*

The passage from Tarakan to Dili, Timor would be as I imagined; it was going to be tranquil enough but the instant I came off the last dogwatch, I took a few moments to sit at the mess table. The few lads there were commenting on the pending 'crossing the line' ceremony. I suddenly had a flash of a memory, of another day I came off watch and sat down at the mess table. I suddenly found myself thinking of the *Furious*. I gave a slight shudder and it was a moment I will never forget in a hurry. Across the table from me was Lofty, a seaman with a grudge against the world. A red-headed Scotsman whom no one thought to cross his path. His hateful nature had a hold on me. He was cutting off a slice of bread with a large bread knife. He looked down his large nose at me and asked me, had I washed my grubby hands before coming onto the mess deck? I had an idea he was just clowning around. I gave a smile and looked down at my hands. He suddenly flared up and all but screamed at me to cut out laughing at him, and before I could get my thoughts together, he let fly the loaf of bread at me. I caught the hard crust in the mouth. Sudden pain from a cut lip was no joke and for the first time I believe I had tears in my eyes from such an attack.

He roared at me, 'Get the hell out of here you skinny Welsh coal-picker!'

That did it, I had a flash of anger of my own to spit out. Without thinking of the nasty consequences from this fiery Scotsman, I yelled back at him to pull his head in, stop flapping his ears and give his backside a chance. There was dead silence on the mess deck. Lofty had been challenged to a rebuff. He lifted up the bread knife and pointed it as close to my bleeding mouth as he could manage without cutting my skin.

'I'll get you for this!' he roared.

But mercifully, he threw the knife across the table and all but leapt out of the mess. If I remember rightly, we never did speak to each other again, and his threat never was carried out. One of the old salts gave me his hankie to wipe the blood from my lips.

COMET CROSSES 'THE LINE'

The ship suddenly resumed its course. We all suspected we were getting close to 'The Line'. Saturday at 0830 13th July, *Comet* crossed the line. The Royal Party appeared near the tubes suddenly from nowhere. They were greeted by First Lieutenant on the Iron Deck, who gave a magnificent low bow to his Majesty (I could see clearly his Majesty was C.P.O. Taylor and he was smiling). The entire Royal Party were in magnificent array as they stood watching the Lieutenant do his stuff. The king suddenly asked the Captain how long had he been holding the exalted rank aboard and why he, the king, had not been informed of any promotion of one of his Royal subjects. The Herald, always quick off the mark had a weak excuse ready to flannel the king. The queen suddenly came to life (who was none other than A. B. Bates — I'll have a great time in pulling his leg over THIS performance). The queen, in such a sweet voice, ordered everyone to the bath (I didn't fancy that). She added, 'Come, Neppy, open up the court.' That was a turn up calling the King 'Neppy', but he didn't seem to mind and so he began to deliver a string of presentation of orders.

The Royal Party seemed to be in a joyful mood until the

punishment of this offender was announced. The axe fell on Anthony Mervyn Hamilton, his rating Rig of the Day and accused of awful conduct, rowdy character, too much leave and was improperly dressed at all times. This ship's member to be so used and dosed with two pills, shaved well, top and bottom and thrown to the bears (the bears being Chief Stoker Reddock, P.O.C. Edmondson, Yeoman Sigs Harper and Midshipman Kidd). The king prayed for silence as the next victim got it in the neck, and my neck was a bit burnt standing there in the sun, but nevertheless it was Sub-Lieutenant Peter Howe R.N.V.R. who was next to fall victim towards the assuring Royals. Subs was accused of winking his gammy eye at one of his Maritime Majesty's subjects, namely a pink mermaid in Mirs Bay, China. Also attempting to induce her to come aboard H.M. ship *Comet* and live in a freshwater tank. A deep breath from the Royal regatta and the king began his sentencing. This crime warrants to be doused with two pills, shaved and ducked thrice.

This next victim was to touch me to the wick. It was the officer over me on the day duty, Sub Lieutenant the Hon. Richard Beaumont. He was accused of appearing on the upper deck wearing his cap back to front thereby causing panic amongst the ship's company by creating the impression that the ship was going the wrong way. His sentence was also a swift one. He had to be dosed with one pill, to be shaved and ducked twelve times. I made a mental note to ask the Sub Lieutenant if he enjoyed the twelve duckings!

By this time, we onlookers began to wonder if there was a chance that some of us ratings were in for a round or two with the Royal Party. They sure were enjoying passing judgement to the upper grades. Time would tell, I suspected, but at that moment it was on to the next victim to flinch under the hammer.

There was a lot of merriment going on as such punishment was being carried out. It was a nice day, and it was a great chance to be able to relax from duties. Even so, the next to receive the axe was the Radio Mismechanic Etherington as his Majesty put it. He had the rating of Value Breaker and his conduct very low and, his leave was to be none because he continued to cause much suffering to the king's loyal subjects by continually beam switching. Also, he was found deprived by winking at the queen. His sentence was going to be harsh I felt that in my bones and very disdainful. The king sentenced him, doused, purged and dunked four times, twice with beam switches up, twice down. Did you ever hear such a roar from the congregation as the suspect was dealt with? We hardly caught our breath when no other than little Boy Signalman Hoffmeyer took his trembling turn under the rueful eye of the king. This lad was accused of flag breaking and his conduct unthinkable, his character vice. Leave time would be spent at Scapa only. I thought suddenly of the time I spent at Scapa Flow aboard HMS *Furious*. Those days were bound in victory for us and the Navy. Life goes on it seems. A loud burst of laughter brought me back to our crossing the line pantomime. Boyishy was found guilty and sentenced to be pilled twice, shaved top and bottom and thrown to the bears. I turned to my mate and said M. B. Collett is making a good barber, must remember that if I want a haircut. I got a dig in the ribs for my trouble just as the king started on his next offender.

Throughout the session of the court, the barber plied his historic razor with commendable skill born of long practice. It is believed that the present barber is the third in a long line of barbers, his grandfather having had the know-how of shaving Nelson when he crossed the line for the first time with the same razor which was used at the present ceremony. The Royal Doctor had concocted a fine line in pills (soap, I shouldn't wonder). Rumour had it that the worthy Doctor himself was made to consume one or two during the execution of sentences.

All through the proceedings the bears gave every appearance of satisfaction with their work and indeed they carried out their duties with zeal and efficiency. It was around about 11.45 when His Majesty, the Queen and the entire entourage went for a dip in the baths — in strict accordance with the long-established customs of the ceremony and assisted by the many hands who were not the King's royal subjects. We took on the merriment for a while, but we definitely were not on a pleasure cruise. It was time to heave to and attend to the matter of the ship. Crossing the line was something special and would be kept in our memories forever and a day. Long live King Neptune and his Gracious Queen.

That appeared to be the end of the ceremony and indeed there were other duties to perform but being such an important ceremony, duties were kind of delayed for the rest of the day. The star players were able to get back to normal and change their colourful costumes for the more convenient dress befitting a member of the Royal Navy and after all we were now on our way to yet another port. I wondered what Dili would be like after the many places we had entered and left. Timor was a place I'm not sure I knew too much about. Getting to pick the brain of our Officer of the Watch might not be to his liking. Some of the crew might have been there at one time or another, but at that moment such things could wait until we actually sailed into the harbour or its equivalent. We could soon find out in a short space of time. Tomorrow might be a surprise anyway.

TO WESTERN AUSTRALIA

After the fun of crossing the line, we were about ready to enter the Port of Dili, Timor. It was expected to be a two-day visit. The crew had hardly settled down to a normal life at sea after the crowning glory of the royal party from the deep. I noticed some of the stars of the ceremony were not too keen to resume life to much after their stint at stardom, but a mattock's life might be kept with both feet firmly on the deck but what a time some of the crew had pulling some legs of the fading stars.

As life would have it, not too much went on at the port, knowing why we stopped there was to re-stock I should wonder, sticking one's nose in the Captain's business was not known in the rules of the sea. Nevertheless, leave Dili we did, and we were all suddenly excited about the trip down under once more.

In late July we arrived in Fremantle, quietly and undisturbed. The weather was to our liking and so were the orders from the bridge that there was leave pending. A visit to a dance club was somehow planned and did we lads who attended have a little harmless fun. I remember the club was called the Havana and life will never be the same again for quite a few of the members of HMS *Comet*. Fremantle and Perth did us proud. Invitations to visit members of the towns and around about were very well received by most of the crew. Some of us were invited to spend a few days in Wingan Wagin and the surrounding townships. We were to test the massive landscape of this huge country by taking the two-hundred-mile trip to that said city. I was invited to a township named Dumbleyung (I hope I remember this is the way to spell these towns). I was the guest of Jack Moran at Dongolocking. A huge sheep station met my gaze, land I thought reached far beyond any horizon I had ever seen. Meeting this family was an extreme pleasure, what a change of life that was for me. I had visions of being able to stay and learn to work the sheep station, a very far cry from the coal fields and the valley of my beloved Wales. Surprise after surprise came and one in particular was what Mister Moran called, I believe, 'a parrot shoot'. This I was not too sure about; shooting these beautiful birds was something, I'm sure, I really didn't relish but not to offend my hosts off to the parrot shoot I went. I understood these birds were really a pest to the community and to the way of life in that part of the country. This was at the end of July. A Saturday night dance at the Dongolocking Hall was a great occasion. The night magically drifted away until 2 am. I had not been up that late since my days on the midnight watch on the *Illustrious*. Now that ship brought powerful memories to me.

Before leaving the Moran sheep station, Mr Moran's daughter, Pat, presented to me a landscape drawing she had painted. It was beautifully done as a ploughed field with trees casting shadows over the scene. I really treasured the landscape and would keep it always as a great time of pleasure the family bestowed upon me.

After that delightful stay, I was a guest of the Wright family. We had been out on a run having a great time, but misfortune took a hand by getting the car bogged on the way back to their homestead. No way could we move the car. A little muddy and still full of fun, we took to walking back home, the two whole miles. On that note, leave came to a very sad ending. At the moment of departure from our new and wonderful friends, I would remember the times spent amongst such grand people and that feeling of wanting to stay in Western Australia which took hold of me. I could not believe how a town on the map of this huge country could affect me this way. Waiting for the train to depart felt like it could be the longest wait of my life. Sad farewells and trying to hide sad faces were a real heartache but at last the train took its leave.

The first day of August found me back aboard the *Comet* at Fremantle. Our time was spent very nicely, the weather was kind but eventually after many days admiring this great city we were sailing off again. This time, destination Singapore. Another tranquil voyage, duties and daily watches to perform saw us safely docked and awaiting further orders. Further orders for me at least came in the news that I was in line for a draft chit for another passage to England. My heart missed a beat, this meant of course that I was to leave *Comet*. Another chapter of my life closing. Little did I know at that moment though, how much of a voyage that was going to be. Even though the turmoil of the past horrible war was still very fresh and cruel to the memory of one and all.

Eventually, on August 12th, we again set sail for Singapore and arrived there on August 19th. At last news of a draft for passage to England, getting there was going to be a voyage of all sorts. The turmoil of after war was still the foremost concern to everyone at the barracks in Singapore and I became the mask of my own destiny. Then it was my twenty-first birthday, the most important day of anyone's life. To celebrate that fastidious day, I was put on duty watch and spent the lonely hours dreaming of parties, champagne, girls and the pleasure of reaching the equivalence of man.

Dream days over and I left Sultan in delightful Singapore on September 18th. I boarded HMS *Formidable* for passage to the UK on September 19th, leaving Singapore on the 21st for Trincomalee. It almost felt like a pleasure cruise, with not much thought of war, however Singapore still held a strong fascination for me. I wonder if the reason was because I had spent my twenty-first birthday there. Of all the dreams I had of when I would be celebrating my coming-of-age shindig, even when I was just eighteen, I often thought of that day. I was told of the antics of my brothers, of whom I had seven, of their coming of age and what they got up to in Wales — very funny things happen on special birthdays. It used to curl the hair on the back of my head to hear some of the goings-on. All these things were part of my very golden memories and on time sharing a lonely pom-pom gun out on the ocean in the middle of the night, there was heaps to think about. All those dreams would blissfully keep me wide awake in case something would come up out of the treacherous cloak of darkness, such as the times when one could sense the presence of floating mines in the cold North Sea. A place far removed from my present and quiet surroundings and I sometimes wonder why we delve on things such as daydreams. I presume we would all like to go way into the future and close the door very quietly on our favourite memories and dreams like this one on my twenty-first birthday. That has taken a lot of filing in the memory bank. Ahead in my journey was the release from the Navy and the thought of homecoming which also would become memories and dreams in the future.

I really did not get much time to respond to the beauty of Singapore, which was our next port of call. I still felt the black cloak of the war upon me. Thinking about my discharge from the Navy, funnily enough made me feel nostalgic. With the very quiet leaving from the *Comet,* my mind turned to the next stage of my disappearing life as a seaman. I was awaiting the orders of my stepping aboard my next assigned vessel but this time for a change it was HMS *Sultan,* a shore base where I was to await a passage to the UK. One bright spot on my calendar was my twenty-first birthday, amongst the slender of the drapes of HMS *Sultan.* Were there parties? Was there champagne? Were there crowds of people to help me become, what was known as becoming a man? 'Not a hope in hell,' I told myself. I simply sat alone dreaming of my twentieth birthday spent in Sydney. There I was among great friends, my dear pal Fred, and Sadie welcomed my birthday and Sadie's family greeted me in style. Looking around me there at *Sultan,* my heart suddenly swore at the war and at the tyrants responsible for it, I really went to town on my misery. I was thinking funnily enough of the saying: twenty-one and never been kissed. Thank God that wasn't true.

A few more days in *Sultan* found me once again on the move and low and behold I scored another ship that was nice and big in the form of HMS *Formidable.* I felt strangely at home on this ship, even though it was more or less in the form of a passenger. Of course, duties had to be carried out and routine to be dealt with as in all Navy vessels but somehow the war was just a ghastly memory. The pacific was still under the veil of violence, I thought, but my part in the conflict was over; *Furious, Illustrious* and *Comet* flashed through my mind, and from boy to man in the space of a number of years. Bells ringing for some order or another wiped the web of sadness from my mind. This ship was, I hoped going to take me home and this aircraft carrier was my salvation. Stopping at Trincomalee was like old times, we were there to pick a number of aircraft. This was a very interesting stay, a very short stay but taking on aircraft was great. The feeling of being back in the fray doctored my wild spirit and I was glad to be at last a little part of it as I was seeing such places as the Suez Canal, Port Said, Malta and Gibraltar. Life can feel wonderful sometimes and on the way to Aden it was to tingle the blood.

Then later on there it was, Aden had appeared on the horizon. Could that sight join the spectacular stage of the Suez, fanciful Port Said and its mysterious goings on, the majestic magic of Malta and the one-and-only Rock of Gibraltar? I was in the throng of pure excitement as I thought of every day that was taking me closer and closer to home. It was really pleasant however, to be at peace on a quiet sea. Thinking of the past and its ugly year of war was not to be tolerated anymore. However, speculation and daydreams were so prevalent that once again a grand sight was to welcome us in the form of Gibraltar. We were really on our last leg of our journey; Plymouth was in our sights.

As I waited the hours away, duty and watches became more than second nature and shipboard life was fast coming to an end. The day of entering Plymouth's welcoming embrace was like music to the soul. My past life aboard all those proud ships was a profound tonic to me. I had taken part in the conflict of a World War and very luckily came out of it without serious injury. I had daydreamed my time away until there it was — Plymouth. That magical town was bathed in sunshine of the early morning. This scene looked so sweet and wonderful, after all it was our home port.

Again, it was time for me to depart yet another ship of the Royal Navy, I was to pick up my belongings and wish the ship goodbye. Departing *Formidable* was just as lonesome as many other ships I had departed but beyond this was the thought of DE mob at the Royal Navy barracks. There would be foreign leave which turned out to be twenty-four days, and there would be a multitude of hugs and kisses from family and friends. The routine of DE mob was going to be chicken feed and I was going to enter my newfound private world with the thought I had tried hard to do my best and emerged from a boy to a man in doing so. There would be bridges to cross and maybe mountains to climb, but like every man that comes home from war there would be change to take as it was dealt out to them.

My entrance into civvy street was really not as I had expected it and it is important to be able to adjust to the new life after the forces. My stop at rehabilitation was to do a course in gas fitting under a government scheme. That life was not really to my liking and it did nothing to improve my health. However, I was saved from this part of my life by a suggestion from a school pal of mine who was still in the army and billeted in private quarters in Earls Court, London. He thought it possibly a good idea if I came to London and sought other employment. The thought of leaving the family again was a bit of a tug of war, so I approached them and told them of my pal's proposal. They gave me their blessings if the suggestion fell into my future plans. My pal told me he could get me 'digs' at the place he was staying. So, with more goodbyes and partings I took my leave and travelled to London where I was housed in the same house as my friend and long-lasting mate, Roy. My quarters consisted of a kind of bed-sit, quite comfortable and from there I commenced to search for a job. To my delight, a job came about in the form of clerical work at the Post Office Savings Bank in Kensington, not too far from where I was billeted. I settled well into taking care of people's savings by keeping their smallish wealth in good order on the records. It did not take long to notice a beautiful girl with that 'page boy' hairdo I so liked in those days. We worked on the same counter and very soon we became friends. She was a smashing girl, full of life and easy to get along with. Our section at the Savings Bank put on day outings by coach which is something we both enjoyed and as time went by, friendship turned into sweet love and we became engaged shortly afterwards.

Some news came out of the blue about an immigration scheme for free passage to Australia for Veterans and their families to migrate. I suddenly remembered the time I had spent in Australian waters. That was aboard the aircraft carrier HMS *Illustrious* in the Pacific waters at the end of the war. A whole new world opened up in my mind. I thought about all of my new friends there and all that sunshine. I spoke to my beloved wife-to-be, Marjorie, about the plan that had suddenly come into being and she was interested to think seriously about such a change of life. We decided if I could be lucky enough to secure a passage that I should go out to Australia and compile a new lifestyle for us, also a home, then Marjorie would follow on the scheme to pay a ten-pound passage because she hadn't served in the forces.

The application was sent and the necessary reply came in due course. A free train ticket and paperwork arrived. I was to travel to Tilbury to join the ship, *The Otranto* at the dock and wait for instructions.

The week before I left for Australia, I took a trip back to my hometown of Pontypool to see the family and to let them know I was returning to Australia on the liner *Otranto* and I was leaving Tilbury on the 4th of May, 1950. There was one other stop I had to make whilst in Wales and that was to visit our famous landmark known as The Folly. It was a very old brick tower standing on the true crest of a very high hill with a commanding view across a wide expanse of Wales. However, during the war this landmark was known to German bombers and it guided their course to the midlands where they reigned terror on the city with their dreaded bombs. So, a drastic decision had to be made concerning the 'tell-tale' Folly and the verdict was that it had to be destroyed, and destroyed it was. So, to that very day, I climbed the steep hillside and the ruins lay in its mass of rubble. I needed to sit amongst the scattered brickwork one more time before leaving for Australia. So, I took myself, alone and full of sad memories and passed the small whitewash public house then passed the very, very old church at Trevethin. Then the mountain stream and up the steep hillside. Just before The Folly, was a very ancient road made of stone slabs by the Romans during their rule over Wales. I stood at the top of the Roman road and my young days flew back through my memory. Then at The

Folly, I sat in the afternoon sun and took a sheet of paper from my side pocket and with a pencil three quarters its size I laid on my stomach and started to write a poem called Folly Lost (I finished it on the *Otranto* on my way to Australia).

The train ride to the dock was exciting and the first sight of the *Otranto* was breathtaking. Boarding at the dock happened quickly and at last a dream had come true. The sail date would remain in my memory forever. It was May 4th, 1950. Confusion was part of departure and excitement was part of the day. At 3.20 in the afternoon we left England.

MY FREE PASSAGE TO AUSTRALIA

RMS Otranto Log, 4 May — 6 June, 1950

First Day — Thursday 4 May
'Tilbury Departure'

Arrived aboard RMS *Otranto* at 2 pm today. Lunch was served at once and at 3.20 pm sailed from the docks. Sea was calm and weather not too bad, everyone aboard busy with first day — aboard duties, group station and dining salon table-numbers given, meeting cabin friends and moving in makes short work of the day. My cabin mates are all bound for Sydney with me which makes us greater friends, some of us have friends at the lovely beaches, one has his friends living in the next street to me. Our meals are really swell aboard, the dishes are too good to be true and everybody is now settling down to a four-or five-week voyage. Smoke rooms and public bars are in great demand. The dance square this evening will be in great demand also. The sunshine is very nice as we slip from the channel and take our last looks at the coastline, everybody will be bent on finding themselves around the ship and as evening falls, we find our first day on board has been one of excitement and very busy. After my hectic day of boarding ship, I took myself to the rail and glanced down at the swirling sea. Suddenly I remembered the same thing whilst aboard the *Furious* in the north of England seeking out the nasty German battleship, *Tirpitz*. How the scene has changed. Here on board the *Otranto* there was no dangerous threat of death or injury and no German dive bombers. Just the sound of the water rushing against the ship. Further along the deck I hear the merry laughter of children out on their voyage of a lifetime. I could dream on about this for hours but the excitement of the day told me maybe sleep might be good after the thrill of the first day at sea. After all, tomorrow is another day.

SECOND DAY — FRIDAY 5 MAY
'ABOUT THE SHIP'
Seven-thirty found our cabin in peaceful comfort but the welcome sight of tea from the steward got everyone sitting up and taking our first cup on our second day. We are all bound for Sydney in our cabin as we keep on telling each other and have already made plans for some nice times when we arrive. Sunbathing in the rays of the sunshine today was grand, everyone seems to love the open deck. A day out from England and the weather has changed a great deal. We have begun to find our way around the ship now and we find the movement of the ship has now been forgotten by most folks, sea sickness has now been shaken off by the first sea voyagers. Tomorrow we will have warmer climate and coastline to watch as land slips behind as we travel towards our new lives in Australia. Afternoon sunshine has been wonderful, we really take the sun as it comes. Evenings find quite a number of people dancing in the square, the bars are very popular on all decks, but we are awaiting the opening of the swimming pools that should be worth the wait. Mealtimes are very welcome, sea air gives everybody that wonderful hunger that has to be seen to at

once, our meals are most agreeable. No one can complain at the smashing service. Tonight has found us late retiring, the evenings are so fresh it keeps us all up and now waiting for our next day at sea. It's now midnight and out goes the lights.

THIRD DAY — SATURDAY 6 MAY
'FIRST WEEKEND'
This morning we had no sign of the sea for a few hours, fog had set in making the weather just like home all over again. We kept to the smoke room and our cabin for most of the time but did spend a few minutes on deck laughing and joking about shipboard life. After lunch, we were back in the sunshine again, the fog had been left behind and once again we were content to sit on our deck chairs and make up for the lost time in the sun. Our first weekend on board was spent like it would have been ashore: dress for dinner, a few hours in the bar and few dances. Everyone seems to have gotten into the swing of the ship's life, the children are having a wonderful time and it is grand to see their happy faces and the way they trip about the ship like old salts. The few I saw that were a little under the weather at the beginning of the trip have now forgotten those few days and are now enjoying themselves to the full. The bar closes at 11 pm, so we have a few minutes strolling around the decks looking at the whitewash left by the trail of the ship breaking through the dark waters, then we stroll back to our cabins and sleep until another day.

Fourth Day — Sunday 7 May
'Sunday Sunburn'

Tea at seven was wonderful this morning, no trouble from a short sleep, been at the bar too long Saturday evening no doubt but the weather is perfect. The sun is shining from a cloudless sky and the recorded sounds of church bells will be rung through the morning. After breakfast, I make my way to the upper decks armed with pen and air mails, I have to get through quite a lot of them before reaching port. I have already got rid of a few and postcards of the ship by posting them at the Pursers office. We sat most of the morning then the afternoon began with a cool drink and played sports for a while. I had a few games of deck tennis with the others and by the time dinner had come around, a few of us were a little cooked. Our white skin had given way to a nice cherry red, a lovely life. A cold shower did the world of good and after dressing we went to the ship's first concert. This turned out very well indeed, the hall was full, and everyone had a really nice time. The end of the concert found us again in the bar, but this evening I settled for tomato juice. A walk around the deck and after watching a storm of thunder and lightning, retired to my cabin at 11 pm. Ending the fourth day at sea and our first weekend, a little sunburned but not sore. One thing of interest to first voyages was passing Gibraltar Rock last evening at about 7 pm. The sailing mileage has been about one thousand miles.

Fifth Day — Monday 8 May
'The Pool'

We awoke again this morning with a lovely sun and yet another nice cup of tea from our steward. We have made up our minds to put away our winter clothing for a while and adopt a cooler dress of sweater and shorts, our fellow passengers have had the same idea. Playing deck tennis again today you can see most of the tropical clothing about. The swimming pool opened this morning and after we had a few games on the top deck we rushed to our cabins, got into our trunks and took the plunge. The water was cold and felt very fresh, just what the doctor ordered, and the rest of the morning was spent swimming and sunbathing. Lunch came and went with the magic hands of time; the food has still kept its real value and we continue to do it justice. The smashing warm weather keeps most people on deck and the swimmers watch quite a few gather around the pool. Most of the afternoon we could see the coastline of Africa in the faint haze of the sunshine, but we kept with it for quite a few hours until after teatime which is at four o'clock. The sun had begun to tell on a few of the passengers by the time dinner came around, the temptation for staying in the sunshine too long was most everyone's devil but I suppose it will be alright in a few days time. My sunburn never seems to worry me, so I take my fill of sunshine. We can all do with plenty of sun now after leaving England only a week behind with snow. The evening found us dancing after swing glass panels were thrown open for the cool evening breeze, a few drinks at the bar and the usual walk along the deck before retiring for yet another day.

Sixth Day — Tuesday 9 May
'Africa'

Today, we had more cloud than usual since we left England but the sun has just managed to shine through. It has been nice for sitting on deck without getting burnt up too much. The children's pool opened up today and what a splash it caused, almost the whole three hundred of them tried it out, they have different times for the non-swimmers, for this the water is lowered for the children to walk about and just get wet. We left our bathing until after lunch, the morning passed with waiting and reading. Our sun tan has become quite colourful now, the sunshine every day has been leaving its mark — sun tan! The coastline of Africa has been in sight for quite some time, the sandy hills and green-tinted fields make quite a picture. The beaches almost stand out white against the blue of the sea, it is quite pleasant to watch. Just before lunch, we passed a liner off on the route we have just taken. I was glad to interest myself in the idea that I was not going the same way. In the afternoon we took another dip in the pool, the cool refreshing water felt smashing. The sea water brings up the tan but the sun has begun to feel stronger now and everybody seems intent on reading and writing out in it. But just before 4 pm, a few spots of rain fell, the first since we left England. We went down to tea and came up on deck to find the sun had found its way out from behind the sad clouds again. A few drinks after dinner, a walk around the deck and I was going to do a few odd jobs in my cabin. Today the clocks went on thirty minutes so I must make that up by going to bed a little earlier. Just before I left the upper deck, a lighthouse was flashing its warning and I suddenly thought of my ships in the war and I really felt rather sad.

Seventh Day — Wednesday 1 May
'Carnival Dance'

Today was the best day to date, at least as far as the heat was concerned. The sun shone from a cloudless sky all day and one can notice the heat has begun to find its way into cabins and covered-in places. The fans should be into full swing very soon. At mealtimes we find the hot breeze rushing around and rushing from the galley in sudden gusts but it really is not much to find uncomfortable as yet. Later, sailing through the Suez and the Red Sea, we shall see more of a change but we will cross our bridges when we come to them. The sweet's queue has at last disappeared, since we left England, most mothers have been standing in great file at the sweet shop, buying much more than they really need. If it has not been eaten by the time we really hit the hot weather, I'm afraid they will have very sticky times with it all. A smashing swim again before lunch, cooling and refreshing but the water is very salty and so clear. We did intend to have a dip afterwards, about 3 pm, but lazing in the sun made us give up the idea so I just went on reading my book, *The Naked and the Dead*, until well after tea. Then we went below to clean up for dinner and the Carnival dance. We received paper hats at our tables, all the trimmings and gay colours and after a few drinks at the bar went to join in the fun. The dance was a great success, they seemed to enjoy it very much. There were a few people still treading the dance floor. I suddenly wanted to go above deck to smell the fresh salty air. Those memories of the HMS *Furious* still haunted me as I climbed up to the upper deck from which the sight of England was nowhere to be seen. The new world was waiting to welcome everyone on board and as always, tomorrow is another day. I returned to the dance room and watched a couple dancing to a romantic tune. A mystery melody suddenly filled my mind as I sat down facing the dance floor and I remembered it was *I'm dancing with tears in my eyes*. I realised that I miss your sweet head on my shoulder. I love you so much, my dear Margie. A sudden voice announced that it was last drinks so with my memories I strolled back to my cabin to await the next historic day at sea. Just after 11 pm, the clocks having to be put on another thirty minutes will make it later again, so to bed and god bless all ye merry gentlemen.

Eighth Day — Thursday 11 May
'P.T.'

The view from my porthole this morning gives a viewing of a smashing day. We were thinking of an hour on the games deck doing a bit of P.T. but the thought of dashing about at 6.30 am was a little too much. It really was a lovely morning, but everything was forgotten, the clocks being put forward and maybe the extra late dance the night before helped us to cover up our shame but anyway we stayed in our cabin until after 8 am. We had a few steps around the decks later before feasting. Our usual sun bath before swimming saw the end of the morning. We did see a little boat drill by the crew just before lunch, very small crew compared to the whole list of passengers. It reminded me of my old Navy days, drilling and lifesaving most every day. The afternoon brought another lovely sunbathing session, our red burn is now beginning to turn a smashing brown. Swimming in the saltwater of the Mediterranean makes the skin much harder and turns the colour to a nice tan. We never seem to get tired of laying in the sun. For a laugh, we did a little comic P.T. in the afternoon, a few of the girls had joined us and we had quite a good bit of fun. Afternoon P.T. can become a very hot and dry bit of work, so after our half an hour of that we all made a dash for the pool and swam about, contented, cool and wet. We stayed baking in the sun till after 6.30 pm, then prepared ourselves for dinner. Afterwards, the dance, never missing a drink at the bar. Everyone has been talking about our first port of call tomorrow. In the afternoon we arrive at Port Said, returning at 11.30 pm. I thought about our notice a few hours ago. Captain's orders were, 'No shore time at Port Said.'

Ninth Day — Friday 12 May
'Port Said'

Today has begun with a very black outlook, the clouds came racing along the sky looking rather gloomy. The sun had been out very early but not many people saw any of it. At around 8.15 am, the ship's loudspeakers broadcast a very grim message: someone had fallen overboard. A few people were at the spot and had thrown a life belt over the side. The person was seen a few hundred yards from the ship when the alarm was given. At once the ship stopped speed and sailed around and around, a few small craft were called to our aid but after an hour no trace was found. The other ships were left to carry on with their grim job. We had to carry on with the trip, we were due in Port Said at 3 pm, but with the delay no one knew what time we would arrive and as if to darken the affair, the storm that had been gathering broke with all its fury. Forked lightning flashed across the sky and thunder bounded through the ship. Within a few moments, down came the rain. People playing deck tennis were partly drowned in the downpour. The rain continued all afternoon. I stayed in the writing room dropping a few lines to friends in Australia. I stayed there until we arrived at Port Said around 4.30 pm, everyone was up on deck watching the sights and all evening afterwards. Traders came aboard selling their wares, silks and trinkets from the East. We had not sailed when I retired at 12.30 am, but there was still plenty of life going on with one thing and the other. We had a midnight kiss from a cup of tea and turned our backs upon the magic of Port Said to await our trip through the canal. We should have passed through most of the Suez in the morning. I hope the weather will be nice again in the morning. God bless the person who died, we were never told who it was.

Tenth Day — Saturday 13 May
'Suez Canal'
I awoke to find we had stopped our engines again, but had moved from our berth of yesterday afternoon. We had already entered the canal but had stopped a little way down, the sandy backwoods could be seen from our cabin. At last we began our trip down the Suez, the day was spent looking at the sights. As usual, we sat on the upper deck after breakfast taking in the views of towns and small dwellings. We passed quite a few of our soldier's camps, and the view from the ship of their quarters looked very nice. The sandy waste turned from rugged space to lovely sandy landscapes. The homes of some of the white people were smashing. Some of the places I had forgotten came sliding into view then slipped away again as we travelled through the sea of sand. The weather has begun to get much hotter now and

after the rains yesterday, the sky has now become very blue again. The water in the canal is a very pale green, so we have not been short of colour with the yellow sand and blue sky. The contrast of the green sea and the blue sky make a beautiful picture. The trip took most of the day and just around sunset we began to leave the narrow waters and turn towards the more open sea. The mountains in the distance showing off their colours to the sudden nightfall and with the haze about the horizon we sailed once more towards open and smooth sea. In a few days we shall arrive at Aden, perhaps we shall be able to get ashore there. It will be our first walk on dry land for fourteen days — time flies. Dancing as usual in the dance square and a few drinks ended a perfect day. Port Said still holds a magic of its own. In war and peace.

Eleventh Day — Sunday 14 May
'The Red Sea'

Morning found us miles from land again and advancing through the Red Sea. The weather has become very hot now and below decks the air has become heavy and hot. The evenings will come as an ordeal from now on, a few people have already begun to sleep on the upper deck. I expect more than a few will be doing the same tonight. The church services are in their stride again today. Our second weekend on board and the bells are very tuneful in the morning air. There is a service for all walks of life. The rain clouds have been shaken off at last and the sky is a deep blue. A few white misty clouds are floating miles up in the heavens and the rays of the sun are pouring down upon the ship giving the searchers of the sun the happiest days of their lives.

The swimming pool has been filled again today; it seems like ages since we last had a swim, but in fact it has only been a day and a half. Coming into Said was the end of bathing until we had sailed clear, something to do with the watch I believe, anyway, we had the most of the swim yesterday and it was very nice to get one's self cool today in the waters of the Red Sea. The day passed without any excitement, but lazing in the sun was ideal for everyone. The pool has been left open until 10.30 pm. I think we shall have to see how time goes on. The heat below decks has become quite a problem but the fans are at work in the smokes' room and bars stirring up the breeze that we are all looking for. The Sunday concert was a little too crowded for me so I took a walk and watched the bathers for a while until the pool closed at 9.30 pm, not 10.30 pm as I thought it would. I sat on deck until midnight, another thirty minutes advanced on the clock then I retired to a very hot cabin.

Twelfth Day — Monday 15 May
'Trottie True'
An early morning swim was the order of the day for quite a few of us as the heat of the night was a little too much. The sea breeze did not help much and the small amount that came through our porthole was lost through the door. The heavy sheets had been removed a few hours before retiring but still the place was very hot. The morning swim came with a very refreshing blessing, but the early morning sun was still burning as we swam through the water. The ship's doctor has warned passengers about sunbathing too much, fifteen minutes is quite the full time allowed per day. Fifteen minutes soon slips around and of course people, not

thinking of the harm that they are causing themselves, just go on laying there in the hot sunshine only to find a few hours later that they are almost burnt to death. It can prove very harmful so I keep to the shade. Our place is behind a lifeboat in the morning and when the sun moves around we get the other side, of course we take our fifteen minutes in the sun, doctor's orders are well worth the while. Mail writing for our friends and family back home took up most of our time in between swimming because we have to have them ready by tomorrow for posting. We arrive at Aden tomorrow afternoon and we can spend a few hours ashore. This evening we saw another film on the upper deck, this time the lounge would be far too hot. The film starred Jean Kent and was called *Trottie True*. A very nice film too, I enjoyed it very much. A short film was also very interesting called *Australian Diary* and of course every family's sweetheart, Minnie Mouse, was shown. No one liked the idea of retiring to their cabins, but still night must fall, people must sleep.

Thirteenth Day — Tuesday 16 May
'Aden'

First thing this morning we were very busy writing our last-minute letters for home before the post closed for Aden. We were due sometime in the afternoon. The hot weather has still kept up with us, but the slight breeze is not enough to cool down the ship. Our gang are still sitting in the usual place behind the lifeboat hiding from the sun, of course when we take our dip in the pool the sunshine bathes us as well. We must get down before our usual time today to get ready for going ashore, we shall have our fun and games until teatime then we get ready for our shore leave. The midday temperature is again in the nineties but now the strong winds cutting across Aden have met us on our way. We spend the afternoon lazing in the smashing head winds, it really is grand to cool off. The hilly landscape has taken the place of sky and sea and the sands upon the hillside are a sight on their own, you have to sit and stare. I can't recall anything looking quite like this. Teatime comes and down we go to get ready. We berth at 5.30 pm and leave the ship an hour after, but not before we all receive our mail. My post had six letters, four I had been waiting for ever since I left my girl at the station in London. Aden was very warm but really full of excitement and gay colours. A few of us went ashore together and had quite a nice evening. The people of Aden are very friendly and have smiling faces and of course the children always steal the picture. We were ashore for four hours walking around looking through the bazaars and shops, having the thrill of a lifetime. At 10.30 pm we arrived back on board and soon after the bells for 'All ashore who's going ashore' sounded and by midnight we were under way leaving Aden and its wonders behind. One more step nearer to our much-thought-of Australia.

Fourteenth Day — Wednesday 17 May
'Head Winds'

The fun of Aden over and done with, we again settle down to our shipboard life. It was really grand to feel oneself walking on dry land again even if the air was very hot. I am sure everyone beyond a doubt enjoyed the open space of land again. This morning found us miles out to sea again with the now usual sight of a clear blue sky. Quite a number of the would-be sun bathers have at this stage of the voyage had enough sunbathing. It really is very strong sunshine and quite a few people have been overdoing it. I have been seeing a number of nasty burns, but the children enjoy it all. It really is a wonderful thing to have these small tots aboard going out to a new world, and a much better one for everyone after our hateful war years. We can all thank God for our wonderful chance of sharing Australia with the Australians. Our early morning swim was grand and even at 7.30 am the sun is very hot. With the clocks being put on every night we are losing a lot of sleep; we are now two and a half hours ahead of English time, but it really is a change to have early morning sunshine. We have land on the horizon this afternoon with great mountains looming up out of the sea, then as we leave them behind, they change into mole hills and disappear from sight from where they came. The film *Trottie True* was shown again tonight for the people who did not see it on Monday. I went to the dance square but got talking to a few friends and did not have one dance. The breeze has now turned into a baby typhoon, lashing the waves around like a millpond on a wet day, throwing the spray along the decks giving everyone in its path a mild shower. I hope it is not the sign of rough weather again, but we must remember, 'wait and ye shall see.'

FIFTEENTH DAY — THURSDAY 18 MAY
'FLYING FISH'
This morning the wind was still blowing itself around the ship in great gusts, whipping the sea into white tufts and catching the spray in its path covering parts of the deck with its wetness. Below decks the heat still holds its ground, keeping all cool in the cabin

is like making toast against a fan in mid summer. We stay along the upper deck most of the daytime to escape the warmth of the ship. It has been ninety-two degrees on the bridge again today and most of the passengers are now taking cover beneath the shade of the promenade decks and smoke rooms and the such that can offer shade. Such a different picture now than the one that could be painted the first few days out, everybody was racing for the sun. Most of us got it too, but some still brave the burning rays of sun. We are now looking forward to the Port of Colombo, we will be having a few hours ashore. We expect to reach the port in a few days. My early morning swim was grand today, the sun had not covered the water with its rays, and we could just feel the coolness of it as we swam around but of course by midday the warm sunbeams had made the pool just warm again. It was still enjoyable in-between letter writing and sunbathing, and just before tea we got very interested in the flying fish that the ship disturbed as it ploughed its way through the ocean. They are funny things to watch, one minute you would swear they were birds screaming across the water until you watch them stop and take the plunge as fish have the habit of doing. We watched for quite a while but the setting of the sun and the new moon took advantage of our sightseeing and gave us a picture to remember always. The colour and beauty of it can only be recorded in paint, writing about it would hide the true picture of such a wonderful sign of nature.

Sixteenth Day — Friday 19 May
'Fancy Dress'

Early morning swim was missed this morning, the heat of the evening was a little too much. There was no refreshing feeling when the steward brought in our early morning cup of tea. The heat was overpowering, one could not sleep and with Captain's orders, every porthole on our deck had been closed because of the heavy winds that had been following us for the last few days. At any moment during the night, a heavy swell may have caught the open porthole and half drowned the lad sleeping the nearest to it. After finishing breakfast at about 9 am, I went up on the upper deck to sit in the cool air of the morning. In about an hour the sun will again be driving the people under shelter. Reading and writing takes up quite a lot of time but the usual lunchtime swim is never let go. Missing one swim a day is quite enough. The flying fish still leap and fly across the bows of the ship, they can be clearly seen by the silver wing as fins in the sunlight which can be seen at a great distance in contrast to the blue sea. The weather was cooler yesterday at eighty-seven degrees but you would never notice it, the decks are far too hot for bare feet. I went racing out a little while ago to find a deck chair but had to rush back after getting halfway up the deck, I almost burnt my feet off. But the shade was so cool. The afternoon saw us visiting the children's fancy dress ball. What a sight, it was grand to see them dressed up to kill, they had the time of their lives and the party afterwards would make anybody's mouth water. I was wishing I would be twenty years younger. In the evening, I went to the dance and had a lovely time with a girl whom I had become friends with at the beginning of the trip. It turned out to be one of my best evenings, thanks to Nancy.

Seventeenth Day — Saturday 20 May
'Race Meeting'

Today will begin our third weekend at sea, it seems ages since we left England and yet again the time seems to have just flown. The hot weather perhaps makes each day seem happier to live through and of course this voyage is just a holiday for all passengers concerned. It really is nice to think that you have the whole day to please yourself how you come to spend it and we all do our best to have a good time. This morning I had the bathing pool to myself, which was very nice indeed. It was about the first time that I can remember that I have had the pool on my own, I really enjoy the emptiness and gave all the time I had to myself for a good swim. Of course, it could not last forever, a few others came in later to enjoy the coolness of the swim before the sun got too hot. The mail for Colombo has to be written and sealed today and tomorrow, then we arrive at the Port around 7 am on Monday. I am looking forward to my mail from home. I have at last finished my novel, *The Naked and the Dead*, after taking eight months to read it, so to make sure of it I am reading it again. It's such a wonderful book and a pleasure to read it again. My pals and I take our 5 pm plunge after tea and have great fun for about an hour, the things a gang can get up to in a pool is just plain silly, but we do have fun. Dinnertime brings lush food again and everybody enjoys it and afterwards at 9 pm we have our first *Otranto* race meeting. Jockeys and owners line up for the start and great excitement reigns over the deck as the shout carrying over the air, 'They're off' echoes. The jockeys start winding their wooden horses along the track. *Just Home* wins. The evening proved very good fun and we had one of our best evenings spent at the *Otranto* cup races and there was a silver cup for the finalist.

Eighteenth Day — Sunday 21 May
'New Moon'

Today we have made up our minds to get all mail to the post before our arrival in port tomorrow morning. So, everybody in my cabin has been at the pen and ink so freedom after breakfast permits. I have long since posted my mail to family at home but am now drafting a few lines to Australian friends. Tomorrow morning, we shall all be looking forward to the fresh mail from home. Lunchtime, we knock off the writing for a quick swim in the pool and then down to dine. The hot sunshine makes you feel rather lazy so in the afternoon we have been doing very little. I could have drifted off to sleep as a few of our crowd did, but I stuck it out — but only for a while. Teatime was a welcome sign as during the afternoon I had been counting flying fish and hoping we were not to have them for tea but no, everything turned out alright. Our 5 o'clock swim was wonderful, the early setting-sun casting colours and shadows over the water and reaching across the pool with the faintest of tints. The cool of the evening makes swimming wonderful and the last rays of the sun tans almost as much as at midday. The new moon is also in the heavens looking like a silver line among the fast-dying rays of the sun. In a half hour the moon will be casting its magic spell over the darkened ocean, it seems to float among the many miles of sky we can see from the sea and looks as it would fall at any minute. A new moon always looks so beautiful, as does this land. Sunday concert had a crowded smoke room and I was too warm to stay, early breakfast in the morning to be ready for going ashore means an extra early night. Colombo should be in sight at 6.30 am.

Nineteenth Day — Monday 22 May
'Colombo'

We awoke this morning and it was almost anchoring time, the warm waters of the harbour were dancing in the early sunlight as we took our first look at Colombo. The weather did not look very promising but at that moment things were not bad. Quite a number of people were already on deck waiting for the first boat to take them ashore. Early breakfast for everyone today because of the shore leave. We let most of the crowd go before us, so while we waited, we had a stroll on the top decks taking another look at Colombo. It was my first look after four years. Before we had finished sightseeing the time was just a little before 10 am, so we made our way to the gangway, getting our passports stamped on the way. We had a grand sightseeing tour of the town before catching a bus for the surf riding beach at Mount Lavinia. The waves are very high but not as big as the ones I have seen at Bondi or Manly. The weather turned out quite warm, we were glad we left our coats on board. I was hoping to get a few gifts for dear friends of mine but as it was in Aden, the price of things was sky high. The limit in money for the voyage was very disappointing but there it is, I shall have to cross my fingers and hope for the best before returning to the ship. The natives of Colombo are very friendly and all smiles but if you let them, they would take your last penny. The short stay went by like magic and we had to be back on board by 3 pm and only just made it. Teatime, we set sail again touching land in eight days which will be our first port of call in Australia. The evenings are quite hot but tonight the wind has begun to play very roughly, and we are running into a swell. Perhaps tomorrow will find us in the calm seas again, the dawning will see.

Twentieth Day — Tuesday 23 May
'On the Town'

Our worse morning since we left Tilbury has dawned upon us, the heavy sea made walking in a straight line almost impossible. The water looks very angry, not to mention that the starboard decks nearest to the water line have been rolled off in case of the heavy swell washing someone overboard. On top of this, the sun has been making a brave attempt to give us another day of sunshine but there are plenty of clouds on the horizon. I hope we are not heading into rain. I managed to get a towel I used at Colombo for swimming washed and dried in the morning sunshine and had just taken down a sweater also when I could see the black clouds racing towards us and before everybody got under cover, the heavens opened up. What rain! That put pay to our laying in the open air for the rest of the day. We made use of the lounge and lower decks port side and spending the afternoon taking in the view of sea and clouds. We stayed until teatime. The evening before dinner we spent in our cabin eating pineapple and coconuts, bought at Colombo. After dinner we saw the film *On the Town*, the colour and music may have been enjoyed better if the rain could have kept off for a few hours but instead we had some heavy showers and had to see the remainder from behind pillar and post, but I enjoyed it in spite of it all. I am not very hard to please. I hope tomorrow will bring the sun out again after these weeks, we seem to miss it very much. To see the decks awash with rain has been something new on the *Otranto*. We only had a few showers the last time we ran into a swell but today has to be crowned 'King', it will take some beating.

TWENTY-FIRST DAY — WEDNESDAY 24 MAY
'CROSSING THE LINE AND FANCY DRESS'

At midnight last night we crossed the 'Line' as the old saying goes and will be on our way to cooler weather soon. Three weeks at sea with very hot weather becomes a bore to some people but perhaps it's because of being on board with only a hot cabin to comfort your sleep. In a few days that will more or less be over and done with. The heavy swell is still running this morning and the black and fearful-looking clouds are racing and pacing across the sky. It does not look like a sunbathing day, but it has not stopped the bathing beauty contest around the pool. It's a good job too, because before it had gone halfway the sun broke through the cloud bathing the beauties in warmth. It was a fine turnout, the girls had pluck enough to parade among all the 'wolves'. It turned out to be a very nice evening — at least for the winners it did. Diving for spoons for the men went on until lunch, what a crowd. The sun stayed out more or less most of the afternoon and towards dinner. All the folks taking part in the fancy dress tripping here and there getting together their costumes for the ball and it turned out to be great. The carnival of fancy dress went through their paces on 'B' deck and were voted the best ladies, gents and best pair. Everybody had the finest time; the band was in top form and the buffet was also swell. There was a fancy feast and it was very well attended, and also Empire Day was spent very well indeed. Queen Victoria was not forgotten, the grand lady's spirit will never be forgotten. We are sailing well into the Indian Ocean now and the weather is hot and the swell is still having its fling. We hit every wave, so it was three days of dancing about the deck. I'm training for ballet.

Twenty-Second Day — Thursday 25 May
'Swell'
Today we have a little more sun to welcome us from our beds. Yesterday we had these dark clouds, quite like being at home again. We also have the swell to put up with again today. This will be the third day of heavy seas and some of the passengers have begun to get very sick with it, of course it does not become very nice for anybody day after day and it seems to be getting worse instead of better. It will have to give up soon. We reach Freemantle next Tuesday, so in any case the poor folks not feeling well will have some sort of rest. I pity them really, it is not a very nice feeling to have day after day but as long as they think about it, the feeling will be there. I find the upper deck has a few more people this morning, the sunshine must be getting them back for a second helping of sunburn. It has become much cooler now, even in the sun. After crossing the line, it will get far cooler each day. We are now rushing on to meet the Australian winter, which is perhaps a good thing too, everybody is beginning to get a little fed up with the heat below decks. It would not be very nice to spend much time below decks in the tropics. I doubt wintertime will give us a chance to recover to take on the summer months of Australia. The high winds this afternoon makes writing almost impossible and of course the swell giving the ship a rumba lesson

does not help much. So, we just let everything go by and take the day as we find it. To be content, or not to be content, that is the question for me. I am enjoying every minute of it. Dinnertime and evening still find us rolling around like a cork, the dancing is a little upset but carries on. It's a little cool tonight so I retire early, 11 pm and another thirty minutes to come off our sleep because of the time difference.

TWENTY-THIRD DAY — FRIDAY 26 MAY
'SWING'

Fourth day of heavy swells and more people are feeling a lot under the weather, quite a few people are ill in their cabins. The fine record we have had since leaving Tilbury in England for nice weather seems to have come to an end. We were saying how lucky we have been up till this week. We really have had three wonderful weeks but now there seems no end to the swell we have streamed into. I bet quite a few people will remember the Indian Ocean for some time to come, and no doubt will be very glad when we berth at Freemantle next week. The high winds this morning have chased the clouds away to give us a very nice day. We have the weather at eighty degrees again but the whole ship is at last cooling down, even the bathing pool seemed very much fresher and most enjoyable. Washing day, and I have picked a fine one, it did not take any time to dry and get a little bleached by the sun. The afternoon was spent reading my usual book, which is the second time of reading it — the writing is out of this world. We did have one small shower but it soon passed off and at afternoon tea we were present at the 'Pig and Whistle' for a jam session. It proved to be quite good too, plenty of swing and a few slow dances for good measure. With the early sunset and fast nightfall, the next thing to do was get ready for dinner, then a stroll on deck which is still very breezy and a little chilly. After the dance tombola, a few drinks for some and the usual thirty minutes on time. We shall soon be hours before English summertime and we still have the same old moon shining for us but also the Southern Cross which is just wonderful and for a change we have a heavy swell tonight!

Twenty-Fourth Day — Saturday 27 May
'Children's Concert'

Our fourth weekend at sea and still going strong. The voyage has been one of good cheer and lots of fun, not forgetting the new friends made en route. We seem to have been sailing for such a long time and still the weeks we have been at sea seem to have flown. I suppose it is the new interest and the leaving behind of winter's snow and the English summer that you have to keep our fingers crossed in the summer in England still, but I know we will all miss the English springtime. But still we can't have everything and Australia holds a new life for all on board, so we must be bent upon making ourselves full in our new homes and for some on board the voyage will soon be over. Tuesday, we say goodbye to those leaving the ship in Freemantle. The usual weather has still to be put up with and each day now the sun is getting colder, it has been under eighty degrees today and even the ship is much more bearable below decks. The high winds failed to stop the children from receiving their sports prizes this afternoon and the concert they put on for we grown ups was quite a success. They were enjoying it with equal joy as the folks that were around. It was quite jolly to watch, and of course afterwards they were taken to have a lovely party tea as only children on a liner could hope to have. The grown ups received their prizes from the Captain at 8.30 pm and after joined in the gala dance. Everybody had loads of fun in spite of the high wind and heavy swell but the lovely moonlight does brighten things up a lot. We are all hoping for a break in the weather before we reach Freemantle and that the rainstorms are getting much better in other words.

TWENTY-FIFTH DAY — SUNDAY 28 MAY
'WHIT SUNDAY'
The lovely blue sky this Whit Sunday morning and smashing sunshine bring back memories of England today. This bank holiday at home is a happy and pleasant one with summertime arriving with leaps and bounds, everywhere you find freshness and a young summer. The weather brought all this back to me this morning, the white fluffy clouds in a dazzling blue sky gives everybody a sign of the holiday spirit. Now the tropics have been passed, the hot burning rays of the sun have been cooled down. It is only just about seventy degrees now. More people are beginning to invade the sun decks again now where it has been far too hot for quite a number of people these last few weeks. With the Australian coast only a day ahead, their weather has just about reached us, by tomorrow I think the weather will be almost beautiful. Today, we have an average English midsummer day and we are all enjoying our last few hours of summer weather before we hit the Australian winter. I have been in my swim trunks all morning getting as much sunshine as I can. The pool

has become quite cold now, my swim was very refreshing but the feel of the trade winds on the wet body reminded me again of approaching weather from winter Australia. Later on in the afternoon, we retired to the lounge on 'B' deck for reading and were not there long before we hit some rain showers which dampened the day's outlook somewhat. They were here to stay for the afternoon, those clouds, and most of the evening. The sky kept hiding its stars and moonlight behind the dark clouds of rain. The Sunday concert went over very well, everyone did their best and afterwards the usual walk to the bow kept the stewards busy until 11 pm. A few more days and Australia will be a part of us, or vice versa.

Twenty-Sixth Day — Monday 29 May
'Storm'

If I have complained about the weather this week, I have not been really meaning it because today has taken the crowning glory. The sea has been very cruel, well at least to first voyagers. The starboard decks are awash worse than ever and all sealed off, a person can hardly walk along the decks, even the glasses on the meal tables have begun to walk about. The swell has turned the sea into mountains and valleys, at times almost leaving the ship in mid-air. The bathing pool was closed down just after 9 am, the water was just too lively to stay in the pool — with every dip of the ship, more water would tip over the side until it had to be closed down. I only saw one lad swimming anyway, it really was a little too cold. The winter has come about us and no mistake a few poor folks have had their fill of this seven-day swell. The doctor has been busy with a few, but tomorrow I hope will see the end of that. Freemantle, I hope, will be kind to us, I hope we have not to wear overcoats and of course the rough sea should be over by then. Most of the day has been spent in the lounge and seeing the doctor, the whole ship has to see him today ready for our first visit to an Australian port overland. Dinner was very nice but the dance has been cancelled because of the storm. So, this holiday Monday will have to be spent as an early night. The bar has been crowded long before dinner, so because of the dance I bet everybody will be taking the booze with them. I shall be retiring early as I don't think the rough weather will disturb me. Ten more days from this voyage will see me in Sydney again. I wonder, how will the rest of the trip go?

Twenty-Seventh Day — Tuesday 30 May
'Fremantle Perth'

After the worse night of our voyage, we sailed into the calm waters of the shaded harbour of Fremantle, our first Australian port. We first sighted land from our cabin's porthole sometime after 6 am and with our usual cup of tea from the steward. We became very active for a rare change in the cabin. We were all out of bed long before seven and by this time we were waiting just off the harbour for customs and doctors to come aboard. We did quite a lot of waiting around to see the doctors and getting our passport papers stamped clear for going ashore. Then we waited for mail, which is of course very important. I received another six, making it eleven to date from my wife-to-be. It really is great receiving mail from home, everybody is always ready for news from home. After breakfast we were off ashore. A quick look at lovely and quiet Fremantle, then a half an hour trip to the city of Perth. The rain, which had been showering down until lunch, cleared up for a very nice afternoon. While in Perth, I managed to see an old friend of mine whom I met while serving with the Navy in Australia. We had a nice chat and enjoyed meeting again. We ended up by looking at the beauty spots of the city. Then we left for Fremantle again and our sailing orders which were at 5 pm, but the rain held the cargo loading and unloading up, so we were quite a while past 5 pm. Evening had brought more rain, but between showers, the almost-full moon shone down her Australian welcome. I hope our journey from here on, with the help of God, will be much better than the last week. Freemantle gave us a very nice day and everybody will be awaiting the second stop and third before most of us reach the end of our voyage. Ten days more and we shall be from the west and into the east and New South Wales. Farewell, Fremantle.

Twenty-Eighth Day — Wednesday 31 Man
'The Blue Lamp'

After our day's rest yesterday from the swell, we thought it may have been left behind but an awakening this morning at sea and all our dreams were smashed. The sky was very dark and heavy with rain clouds and that loving swell had made a point of keeping company with the ship. The air has become quite cold now and as we sail past the rain-swept west Australian coastline, the warm clothing has begun to come out again. You sure do see some different changes in the weather in these Australian waters. Just two weeks ago, we were lounging about in swimsuits and shorts in ninety-four degrees in sunny weather, and now, we may as well be in Iceland in mid winter. Most of the day we have sat in a sheltered spot by the bathing pool, watching the coast as we travel towards our next port of call. The high waves could be seen quite clearly bashing against the rocks, throwing spray high above the sea level. The sun came out for a few minutes at a time in between showers, but as teatime came around, we had a very nice date with a film just after the meal. The film has been a great hit in London, where I failed a few times to get in to see it. The much-talked-about *The Blue Lamp* has been a success aboard the *Otranto*, also, the fine acting made the film a very interesting story. I enjoyed it very much, and it made most people at the show forget the wet and stormy weather about us. I was so glad to hear the film was aboard, I have been very lucky in not seeing any of the films in England. People do get a lucky break sometimes. Tonight, the prices of wine and shop goods have gone up to Australian control, most people will find a change. On goes the clocks another thirty minutes.

Twenty-Ninth Day — Thursday 1 June
'Australian Bight'
Our morning cup of tea comes around these mornings while it is still dark. We notice it very much after the early dawn and the shining sun was coming through our porthole only a few weeks ago. The wind has a nip that makes one think of another winter ahead, after just leaving one behind but still, for the first of June and of course mid winter the weather has not been so bad. To be thankful in saying the sea today is lovely and calm, the sun is out in an almost clear sky but not so hot as it has been. It is very good to see the nice weather again because the large swell on the sea was making moving about the ship very uncomfortable.

Today everybody has been taking in their fill of nice weather again. It has been about ten days since we have been able to enjoy the voyage as we have been today. Ever since we left Colombo a week last Monday, it has been very grim as far as laying in the sun has been concerned, but still I hope the bad weather has been left behind although we were expecting to get our worst weather sailing though the Great Australian Bight but in fact so far it has been our best days for over a week and we are well over halfway through. I hope the ship will be lucky enough to make good sailing all the way now, then Adelaide will be reached the day after tomorrow with God's will and a fair sea. Then not many days before we say goodbye to 'home' as we have grown to call the *Otranto* in the last month. Our sailing time from Tilbury has been four weeks today, and another one to go before Sydney. Tonight, we hold a gala dance and fun will be had by all, most people seem to love the dancing aboard ship. Must be the fact of the voyage still fresh in our minds but we must not forget the usual thirty minutes tonight. Must be hours ahead of life by now.

Thirtieth Day — Friday 2 June
'Rain'

At last our record of sunshine has been broken, I thought with the dark clouds yesterday we would have had our worst day of the voyage as far as sunshine was concerned but today has changed all that. From the moment we awoke this morning, the sky has been overcast with very heavy rain clouds blotting the view and horizon right out, for a few minutes we could see parts of the horizon but most of the time the rain was making short work of the view. It came down in large drops, splashing the decks with such strong beats that for rest of the day that was how our day was lived. Not a sight of the sky since early morning, it had been well-hidden today. I am wondering about going ashore tomorrow in Adelaide, it will be a fine thing to be sightseeing in the rain. It will make our visit a bit unpleasant, but we must cross our bridges when we come to them. Perhaps we will be surprised as we have been about the Great Australian Bight. The tales of rough weather we would encounter were much overdone. Our last two days have been the best since leaving Colombo. Today's sailing has been calm and peaceful and if the sun would have been shining it would have been beautiful, but then again, we must be thankful for small mercies. We have almost sailed across the Bight now, and tomorrow we arrive at our second Australian port of call. Some more of us are disembarking tomorrow, so we are having a last drink in the bar. The best of spirits go with them and happy landing in a new land and hoping we all shall remember our voyage together to Australia as the years roll by with sweet memories.

Thirty-first Day — Saturday 3 June
'Free Adelaide'

Today was another big day in our lives, the visiting of our second port of call in Australia and I must say we were not disappointed in any way. The city seemed so alive and free one had the feeling of being a part of the city itself. I think everybody had a good time, not even the rain could spoil our day ashore today. It was lovely to wander around the shops and look at all the things we missed in the war, but still good old England has not been doing so badly. She has come up smiling again, I shall always be proud to say I was born in Britain no matter how long I live abroad. Everyone would do the same no doubt, to feel that way about the land of their childhood. We arrived in the harbour about 8 am and without much mishap we got alongside the quay and were all ready to go ashore. A special train took us to the bit from the outer harbour in just thirty minutes and we soon got down to the sightseeing. The well-planned streets and the ever present no-hurry-way of getting about one's doings were just wonderful after living in busy London. I found it a great change to take things easy in the city and everybody seems to have a smile for you. The charm and grace of free air in Adelaide will be remembered by me for many a long day. Our sailing time was 3 pm and the time soon buzzed by. I tried to find a friend of mine while we were in town, but he had moved out not leaving his forwarding address. I last saw him in London in September 1949, perhaps we may meet someday. The rain gave us a send off at 3 pm and quite a number of people collected to see their friends on board off. A few more of our number have now departed to begin their new lives here in South Australia. One more stop and we will be at the end of our long journey. We will miss the thirty-minute advance when we leave the *Otranto*.

Thirty-second Day — Sunday 4 June
'Southern Australia'
This morning we have the weather somewhat brighter than it has been of late. The sun has been shining through a mist most of the early hours but now, after finishing breakfast, the heavy clouds have begun to break away leaving the blue sky for a few minutes and giving us a little time in the still warm sun rays. The wind

is mighty bitter here along the coast, something warm to wear is really needed if one intends to stay in the open air. We are sailing near the coastline now of South Australia, we will do this more or less from now on until we reach Sydney. We have one clear day of sailing before we reach our last port of call before New South Wales. Melbourne will be our last stop, then we set sail after three days for our future home port of Sydney, arriving on Friday morning. The coastline we have been passing all day today has been rather beautiful in its own way. The many coloured rocks along the rugged beaches could be seen quite easily and the heavy surf pounding upon the thousand and one rocks could be seen covering the whole cliffs with spray. We could almost imagine the thundering sound the waves caused as the rollers went racing towards the land. Most of the day the sun had been playing hide and seek with the clouds which were gathering more thickly by the time teatime came around. Darkness fell with a heavy belt of dark clouds racing along the western sky, no doubt in time to welcome us into Melbourne with the wetness of the last two ports, but still our visits have been wonderful. My first visit to Melbourne will come tomorrow, I hope the weather will be kind to us at least for one of our days in the city. The mail this morning was quite welcome again from home, it's a wonderful thing.

Thirty-third Day — Monday 5 June
'Melbourne First Day'

Very interesting sights awaiting our view this morning as we entered Port Melbourne. The skyline was very nice indeed. The early morning light was not too far advanced as we were coming alongside. We could see the million and one lights of the harbour as we drew alongside the landing stays and wharfs. We ate breakfast and went upon the upper deck to find the air bitter cold and for all the world like England in December. The grey sky had been trying to give us a little more rain, but the breeze was a bit too strong and kept hustling the dark clouds on their way before too much trouble was caused. Quite a lot of working was underway in a very short time after we had docked with the unloading of baggage and sacks upon sacks of mail. Quite a lot of people have now left the ship and while we are in harbour we have only one meal sitting instead of two. Many of the passengers are away for a while on shore. We sail at 5 pm on Wednesday, June 7th. We stayed aboard until after lunch at 12.30 pm (new time) then went ashore to have a look around Melbourne. We did not do very much sightseeing but what we did find was very impressive. It really is a lovely city, well and truly planned and some very fine buildings towering into the winter sky. What we missed today we can see the next day and the next, weather permitting of course. We had to land in the middle of a rail strike with no trains running but it was only a few minutes run by coach to the city itself from the harbour. So, we were not troubled very much. The rain has tried to dampen the place most of the day but without much success. We managed a walk across the beach while waiting for the bus and were back aboard in time for dinner and down to a little writing. Friday seems such away from now!

Thirty-Fourth Day — Tuesday 6 June
'Melbourne Second Day'

This morning was very cold indeed and as regards to our cabin we were not at all in the mood for our early breakfast. All the mealtimes had been put an hour forward while in harbour, so this makes our breakfast time 7.45 am instead of 8.45 am, making us lose an hour's sleep, or rather lay in. We still managed to brave the cold winter's weather and find our way to the dining saloon 'if it was middle night' but afterwards by going up on deck I discovered it was not half as cold in the morning as it was below decks, and making things much better, the sky was clear of clouds and the mellow sun was shining upon the decks once again. I strolled along the deck for almost an hour before returning to the cabin to find that some of the lads had gone back to bed. What a life. Almost five weeks of rest and holiday on board and they have to go back to bed, boys will be boys! The lovely sunshine gave me the walking habit so I went strolling along the harbour beach until lunch time. I enjoyed it very much and took in the way of living as far as I could gather from where I was walking. Most of the people still seem to take life as it comes along, no hurrying, all in its own time. What a wonderful people, these Australians. Afternoon finds me and one of the lads from the cabin down in the city taking in the sights again, everything is so gay and full of life. Shopping would be such a treat here, my girlfriend would love this very much, she will soon find out when she arrives in Sydney from London to marry me, lucky guy! Melbourne is really a nice city, and to end our trip today before returning to the *Otranto* we saw a really smashing film at Melbourne's Savoy called *Morning becomes Electra*, wonderfully acted by all the cast, and after back to our cabin for a private drink. What did we drink? Why rum, of course.

Thirty-Fifth Day — Wednesday 7 June
'Melbourne Third Day'

A wonderful surprise befell us today because a friend on board had found a great friend of the family in Melbourne and had wanted us all out on a toast of the city and outer parts of the bush. The people were owners of a printing and paper works and were quite high in the trade. The offices were in the city and we were in a party of six with the owner's car for the day. Our driver was the boss's right-hand man, very nice people and with his wife we were a nice crowd. My mate in the cabin came, also a girl who was lucky enough to have the friendship of these nice folks and my other shipmate. Everything was perfect, the day was smashing. We toured Melbourne and the ranges, stopping just outside for lunch at a mountain roadhouse. The expenses were all paid for, what wonderful people we have come to in Australia. Arriving back on board just after four, we showed our friends over the ship and came across the notice: '*Otranto* will sail at 9 pm instead of 5 pm'. We were overjoyed at a few more hours with these people, but they had to leave at five-thirty to take the owner's car to the office. But more friends took us to their homes afterwards for a farewell drink. Everybody had a smashing time. Mr Brown, our driver, took us to the house before saying goodbye. Wonderful people. We arrived back on board at 7 pm and after a wash and brush up, we went to the lounge for a few drinks to give cheer to a wonderful city and its grand people. I shall always remember Melbourne for its grand people. Our send-off was a smashing sight, streamers flying from the ship to the shore. Quite a time was had by all and the crowd was very heavy on the quay. The decks of the PO liner *Himalaya* berthed alongside us, were also crowded watching us depart. Farewell, Melbourne.

Thirty-Sixth Day — Thursday 8 June
'Last day at sea'

This is our last complete day at sea, our wonderful voyage is rapidly coming to a close. It has been a great adventure to look back on in the years to come. All the friends we have made and all the folks we lived with through our five weeks at sea have been great to one and all. I have seen wonderful times in my Navy days, but the memory of this voyage will live with me for the rest of my days. I shall always regard the *Otranto* as a part of me and the swell memories having been made while I was aboard, but all good things come to an end and tomorrow we all start a new life. This morning has really been great, the sun has been quite warm, and the usual blue Australian sky has been kind to us on our last day. A lot of clearing up has to be done with Government Official forms to fill in and interviews of small matters, packing of cases and news of what has to be done when we go ashore tomorrow. Afterwards, I had a nice rest on deck in the warm shine of the sun until lunch and then the morning was over. Then we teamed up with friends, my mate and I from the cabin, for a game of deck tennis and played for most of the afternoon and enjoyed ourselves very much. I also spent some time working out about jobs in Australia which brought us to 4 pm and tea. Evening saw us enjoy our last film aboard called *My Favourite Blonde*, quite funny and full of life. The evenings are very dark but we can still make out the outlines of the coast in the not-too-far distance. Every now and again we can see the warning flash from the few lighthouses along the lonely beaches and with a cool breeze the evening says goodnight and we retire for the last time aboard the *Otranto*. Sydney tomorrow!

THIRTY-SEVENTH DAY — FRIDAY 9 JUNE
'SYDNEY'

The last day of my thirty-seven days at sea, 9 June 1950. At last our day has arrived and by the time the morning sun was up, everybody had arisen and where wide awake trying to get the first sights of Sydney Harbour. The sun has made the morning beautiful and the weather is quite mild. Breakfast was early and customs were to be seen and passed before we berthed at the quayside. It was just after 9 am when the gangway connected us to the land again and a little while after when our friends were allowed aboard. Everybody was full of smiles and in the best of spirits as each person received their friends. I had two very dear friends to meet me, and the welcome I got I will never forget. We were kept about the custom sheds for a while though, getting our luggage unloaded and passed by the custom officers. I managed to get most of my things cleared before the dock workers knocked off for lunch. So, to kill time we were taken to Kensington for our ration cards and a light lunch. Then back to the sheds, but my last piece of luggage had not been brought up, so we took what I had to my new home with my friends. I later went back in the afternoon to collect the rest of my things and get them passed. It took me another three hours to get there and back but at last everything was done, and I began to settle down with my dear friends again. The city looked the same, the house was just as nice as home from home and now my voyage is at an end. I begin a new life in a land of plenty. My luck depends on my good health and the will to work.

FOLLY LOSS

I sit on the hilltop alone and contented
The warm summer sun moulding my dreams
I slip back in memory to days that were troubled
I think of the landmark destroyed there by schemes.

I wander alone in dreams of my childhood
The landmark I used for a rest to my back
Its name was 'The Folly' a towered construction
It dominated the scene for miles of the track.

The black clouds of war invaded my homeland
All the fit lads marched off to the war
I sat on the hilltop counting my daydreams
I then turned my back sadly locking the door.

I travelled far and I sailed the blue ocean
Sharing the dangers with millions of boys
My faith in God and in folk left behind me
Was always the answer when death marred our joys.

Letters from home were fresh and delightful
No words of sorrow no lines of remorse
I always had news of my retreat on the hilltop
Then one day disaster struck to alter the course.

I read as I sailed the flamboyant ocean
Of the sacrifice imposed there on the hill
Too conspicuous a marker for enemy bombers
My landmark was blasted to spoil the Hun's kill.

A pacific rendezvous was my immediate future
The news from home held excitement at bay
I engaged my thoughts to the crest of the hilltop
Forgetting the Japs I would face come the day.

Indigo sky from a star bannered heaven
The moonlight gleaming on salt crusted steel
I wait at my pom-pom ready for action
Determined to battle with thoughts far too real.

After the war years silver linings glow brightly
Peace in our time brought joy and the tears
The warriors returned to their own humble castles
I wandered back home to face my own fears.

Bomb scares created on our proud homeland
A weary population facing life with a smile
Throughout my sojourn I had pride as I waited
To view my hilltop and dream for a while.

Summer skies greet me like Australia's blue
White clouds jump the hue like the crest of a wave
I sent out on my pilgrimage on that familiar road
To find out what dreams from the war I can save.

The church at Trevethin still stands as years long ago
The weather cock on duty weathered the storm of the war
Those calls from the golf links I remember I've heard
Then on top on the crest is the loss the town saw.

I pass through the laneway so peaceful and still
I cross the small bridge as I did as a boy
I pause for a moment before climbing the hillside
I wished for the days that were so filled with joy.

Halfway to the summit the horizon grows near me
But the scene I remember will not be the same
I prepare for the damage the view will soon show me it's
Folly Lost I've given the rubble a new name.

Yes the skyline is marred by the hillock of rubble
No tower leaps up from the scene it once graced
Just a plain old horizon the wind whispers the loss
I stand there in silence for the memory I've embraced.

I move not a muscle my mind fails to respond
The wind tried to tell me, face the changed land
I stare down in the no sign of these times
We need a new Folly and here it must stand.

I find myself walking to the spot I hold dear
I try to look into the world still to come
I suddenly know all the past is behind me
So was my youth like the last sound of a drum.

I stand near the ruin just looking around me
Nothing has changed but the Folly's straight line
Under my feet where I now stand and gaze from
I hope the rubble will gather and again look so fine.

I sit on the hilltop alone and rejected
The warm summer breeze moulding my dreams
I have passed the years on my memory excursion
Will Pontypool be changing its future schemes?

Now we are free as the sky over my hilltop
 Let us all march to the future with pride
I dream of the day when the Folly is standing
Whilst the memory of yesteryear might be turning the tide.

I stroll from the hilltop alone and contented
I picture a paddock alive with sweet corn
I know one day my wish will be granted
The pride of Ponty as the Folly's reborn.

IN AUSTRALIA

I had arrived in Australia and for a while I stayed with friends at Ashfield. My other friends, the Rogers family, gave me the good news that Marjorie could stay with them until such times as we could find a house or apartment. The glorious day arrived when my darling set foot on Australian soil. What a meeting! The Hall family, the Fraser family and the Rogers family joined me in welcoming my love to Australia.

Life was a ball from that day onwards. We decided to stay with each of our friends for a while until the time would come when we could properly take up house. I found a job with Fred at a shoe factory and Marjorie found one at Singers sewing machines in the office at Crow's Nest. I must say, those few months ahead of us were very hard to take, with our working in different suburbs and living apart, life did take on a shady tilt. We did manage to spend weekends away at different places, for one we spent time with the Frasers in the Blue Mountains. As time went by, a spot of luck came our way and Fred and Sadie told us of a small apartment in the next street to them in Croydon which was vacant, and of course we took it. Good luck comes to everyone who waits and our newfound home was a small delight. Resumed friendship with Fred and Sadie was a godsend to Marjorie, who until then had no acquaintances in Crows Nest except our dear friends, the Rogers family. Life seemed full of roses for us in our newfound home and Marjorie had settled into life in Australia very well. We spent lots of time with Fred and Sadie, and one summer the four of us planned a holiday at a beach further up the coast. Time to depart drew near and then one evening we received a phone call from them asking us to come down to their house for a chat and drinks. News of tremendous happenings came about; Sadie had become pregnant and thought a trip up the coast would not be wise. Marjorie and I were overjoyed at this news and relayed news of our own which we were very reluctant to tell them. Marjorie was also pregnant, and with everyone overjoyed we cancelled the trip.

The result of these pregnancies was that Marjorie presented me with a daughter whom we named Janet, and a few days later, Sadie had a son named Geoffrey. Days of roses and honey followed, and families and friends were overjoyed. Later on, we encountered a problem with our small apartment, but we were lucky enough once more to gain the help of friends at Glebe which was very close to the city. They knew of a larger apartment close to where they lived, they also had a small shop a few doors down. After settling in, I received some bad news that my job at the shoe factory was to be abolished but the sun was really shining on me as I soon found a position at a hat manufacturers in the city. I'm glad to say that job was to last twenty years, but in the meantime, there was another addition to my family in a second daughter whom we named Linda. With two daughters to look after, once again the apartment became too small and back to the drawing board so to speak. Again, luck was on our side and a charming house was found in the suburb of Chester Hill. I found a position as a civilian clerk with Royal Australian Air Force at Regents Park, where I stayed for another twenty years, and meanwhile between those years, a third daughter was born to us whom we named Joanne.

There it is, life had come full circle because close to Chester Hill is Warwick Farm, so here I am standing close to the replica of the Sydney Harbour Bridge gazing at the racecourse where so many years ago I changed from a young boy to a very proud man. Casey brought me out of my dreaming as we entered the village by calling out that we were standing over lots of yellow fish and as I looked down, sure enough there they were. A stream ran through the display village and somehow they were beneath our feet so Casey and I stood for a while looking down at the goldfish and other larger fish. The office staff were pleased to see such a young visitor to the display village and we were given a glossy booklet covering the homes that were on display. Casey lives in Ruse, near Campbelltown and was used to a lovely home but walking around these grand display homes seemed to please her to no end. Before we passed through the office onto the roadway, leaving the village, Casey smartly said that when daddy came home from work that day, she would ask him to come back to the homes and fish for some of the goldfish because there were so many and the lady behind the desk wouldn't miss about three. God, how I love that child.

Escaping through the war was a blessing in itself to me. I had come full circle since those days when I was eighteen. I must remember to look once more from one of the homes displayed across from Warwick Farm Racecourse. Casey did tell me to do so, didn't she?

THE END